Multicultural Theatre

SCENES AND MONOLOGS FROM NEW HISPANIC, ASIAN, AND AFRICAN-AMERICAN PLAYS

edited by
ROGER ELLIS

MERIWETHER PUBLISHING LTD.
Colorado Springs, Colorado

Meriwether Publishing Ltd., Publisher
P.O. Box 7710
Colorado Springs, CO 80933

Executive editor: Theodore O. Zapel
Cover design: Tom Myers

Library of Congress Cataloging-in-Publication Data

Multicultural theatre : scenes and monologs from new Hispanic, Asian, and
    African-American plays / edited by Roger Ellis. -- 1st ed.
            p.   cm.
        ISBN 1-56608-026-6 (pbk.)
        1. Acting--Juvenile literature. 2. Monologues--Juvenile literature. 3. Dialogues
    --Juvenile literature. 4. American drama--20th century--Juvenile literature.
    5. Minorities--United States--Drama--Juvenile literature.   I. Ellis, Roger, 1943
    May 18-
    PN2080.M88   1996
    812'.5408--dc20   96-22150
                                                                              CIP
                                                                               AC

        2   3   4   5   6   7   8   03   02   01   00   99

for
Rose, Jeremy, Alex, and Josh

ACKNOWLEDGMENTS

In editing this anthology of new dramatic writing, I am indebted for the assistance of numerous groups and individuals who made the book possible. First of all, credit must be given to Grand Valley State University for its financial support of my project, and for my one-semester sabbatical leave when it came time for me to make all the final arrangements for preparing the manuscript for publication. I must also recognize the contribution of the Los Angeles Public Library for facilitating my search for new scripts. Mr. Tom Harris, Editor of the Library's Audrey Skirball-Kenis Theatre Play Collection, was instrumental in placing me in contact with many of the authors whose plays are represented here. Finally, I am also indebted to many of the agents and authors who helped me in locating new work, cooperated with me in arranging permissions and fees, and whose advice on editing selections and writing the prefatory material was in many cases very useful.

Contents

INTRODUCTION

Multicultural Playwrights and the Contemporary American Stage

One of the little known success stories in our nation's painful history of race relations is the nurturing and development of multicultural theatre forms, artists, and institutions over the past thirty years. Beginning with the Ford Foundation's support for the Negro Ensemble Theatre and its artists in the 1960s, and continuing down to the present with the emergence of such groups as the East-West Players, the St. Louis Black Repertory Company, or the Repertorio Español (to mention only a few institutions), the growth of multicultural theatre in the U.S.A. has been rapid, pervasive, and artistically invigorating.

Certainly no other nation can equal the number of new plays and new writers that the U.S. has produced in the past three decades; even the output of our motion picture industry — despite its golden glitter — is dwarfed by the sheer volume and quality of new writing pouring out of our playwrights and taking to the boards of our playhouses. Multicultural authors are no exception to this explosion of talent: the American theatre, healthier now than at any other point in its history, has found ample room for the new voices of African, Hispanic, and Asian-American authors writing of our collective experience. Whether mainstream and "uptown" in their thrust like David Henry Hwang (*M. Butterfly*), or on the cutting edge of literary/theatrical experimentation like Suzan-Lori Parks (*The America Play*), these emerging playwrights have carved out distinguished places in our American theatre, and the future promises even larger audiences for their talent.

The record is not perfect, of course; surely much remains to be done and numerous uncertainties abound on the road ahead — financial, cultural, aesthetic, political. Voices on the left decry continuing racism that sometimes prevents more theatres from producing ethnic works, while voices on the right bewail the strident ethnocentrism that threatens to impede multicultural assimilation. But who would assert that writers like Maria Irene Fornes, August Wilson, Jose Rivera, David Henry Hwang, or Luis Valdez are any longer relegated to the ethnic sidelines of dramatic effort? Their work and that of dozens of their colleagues has established ethnic theatre as a vast and vital genre invigorating the all-too-familiar repertoires of our mainstream, Eurocentric, and largely "white" professional stages from New

1

York to L.A. Although some of our theatres and their audiences may still be slow in responding to the pluralistic demographic trends sweeping the country and creating a new national identity, the transformation to a multicultural society is well under way in most of our playhouses, largely as a result of the growing work of ethnic writers over the past two decades.

This anthology attempts to reflect and celebrate some of the major features of these writers over the last ten to fifteen years. It takes as its subject plays which deal in some form with the confrontation between traditionally Eurocentric, Western values and those of other ethnic cultures, either here at home or internationally. It is not meant to be — nor can it be — definitive because the arena is too large, the crosscurrents too disparate, and the growth rate too unpredictable to be adequately contained within the pages of a single volume. Already, however, we can identify some of the major contributions the writers contained in this book have made to our contemporary theatre scene, and hopefully this collection will highlight some of these for readers.

Of central importance in appreciating these playwrights is the degree of public awareness of ethnic issues and concerns that Asian, African, and Hispanic-American authors have generated. Too often such topics capture our attention only when polarized groups erupt in urban violence, or when TV talk shows require fodder for shallow soundbites and slogans. But these can never substitute for intelligent discussion. At a point in our nation's history when intercultural communication too frequently breaks down and racial issues threaten to explode in practically every large city, the work of these writers becomes extremely timely. They have led the way in identifying for our society racial issues in need of attention (prison reform, discriminatory immigration policies, the spread of AIDS in ethnic communities, etc.); and their plays provide audiences with the background, insight, and "lived experience" that can lead to solutions for social conflicts.

A second contribution of multicultural playwrights that must not be overlooked is the authentic, grassroots nature of their creative efforts. More than any other group in the American theatre, it is the Asian, Hispanic, and African-American writers who have "discovered" the stage as their medium of choice in a media-saturated society. Compared to budget-busting film and television, producing significant work for the theatre *is* still financially within their reach. In fact, it just may be because the theatre *is* so impoverished, that it no longer appeals to the dollar-hungry moguls and fame-driven celebrities crowding our TV, motion picture, and recording industries. Dramatic art, that is, seems to lend itself nowadays to those seeking satisfaction in aesthetic, cultural, or political terms rather than in financial ones; and to those who reject the cultural stereotypes and conventions of Hollywood. Thus, in a society which often seems obsessed with wealth, image, and fame, the stage remains a low-tech alternative that offers emerging writers of color significant imaginative freedom.

Finally, one must certainly take note of the strictly theatrical contributions that multicultural playwrights have made to contemporary American stage practice. Vigorous writing by Marion McClinton, Anna Deavere Smith, George C. Wolfe, Eduardo Machado, Philip Kan Gotanda, and many others has challenged the imagination of some of our finest designers, directors, and actors. Caridad Svich, Richard Nelson, Naomi Iizuka, and others have "pushed the envelope" of dramatic structure in order to reveal new possibilities for storytelling and plot development. And the unique historical perspectives found in the plays of Wakako Yamauchi, Charles Smith, and Migdalia Cruz, to mention only a few, have catapulted into the spotlight the lives of Japanese, African, and Hispanic people, and infused the modern American repertoire with a gallery of stage characters never glimpsed before in such bold relief. Our theatre is certainly the richer for these contributions.

Multicultural Playwrights and the Politics of Race

It is impossible — and perhaps even unfortunate in some ways — to speak of these authors without at some point placing them in the context of their ethnic backgrounds. The adjective itself, "multicultural," seems to set them apart as "not just ordinary playwrights"; and while to some artists this is a welcome situation, to others it suggests a denigration of their talents. Certainly within the current climate of our racially charged nation, the adjective has become so overworked that its precise meaning remains fuzzy, especially to those who bandy it most frequently. But use it we must if we're to understand the important cultural upheavals now taking place around us in our society. And for purposes of this anthology we must also examine a few of the word's definitions and the theories connected with them in order to understand the racial politics which infuse so much of these writers' work.

One of the most common notions of "multicultural theatre" holds that many ethnically distinct writers, plays, and institutions can coexist within the same artistic arena at the same point in time. To some extent this is an accurate description of theatre here in the United States. Just as this book singles out twenty-nine writers for special consideration — and even subdivides them into three distinct ethnic camps — so too one can point out the special talents of the Teatro Campesino or the East-West Players, and distinguish between the uniquely different subject matter found in the plays of Kia Cothron and Jeannie Barroga and Karen Tei Yamashita. All of them — artists and institutions — coexist and continue to be major forces shaping the development of the American theatre at this point in its history.

Unfortunately, though, this model doesn't take us much farther than racial classification of the playwrights when it comes to understanding the range of these authors' talent. Nor does it explain much of the enjoyment audiences derive from plays by Carter Lewis or Rick Shiomi or others, except when those writers are concentrating on strictly ethnic conflicts in a given play. And few of them wish to do that, to write only for a small ethnic coterie of the like-minded. Audiences, after all, are not moving down an "ethnic buffet line" when they come to the theatre, sampling a little of this and a little of that like tourists stepping off a cruise ship for a few hours in one exotic port after another. While this may have been the case twenty or thirty years ago when little or no theatrical attention was paid to ethnic concerns, and when ethnic writers were helping to establish some sort of cultural identity and presence mainly for their own enclaves, it certainly no longer holds true today.

The "coexistence" or "salad bowl" model of multiculturalism also suffers from its inability to identify the creative sources from which these artists draw their inspiration. While these authors' ethnic backgrounds certainly account for much of the subject matter contained in their plays, and even provide many playwrights with innovative stage techniques, it's impossible to ignore the dominant Eurocentric influences upon the form of their work. Shakespeare, for example, as well as Brecht and Artaud, figure largely as creative stimuli in the backgrounds of many of these writers of color; and to ignore this fact is to delimit these playwrights' achievements both as artists as well as ethnic artists.

A second popular notion regarding the term "multicultur-

4

alism" in the United States is the theory of the melting pot: the notion that all ethnic groups in our nation will eventually be assimilated into the Eurocentric, white-dominated, cultural mainstream. Like the "coexistence" theory just described, this too seems an accurate, though partial, description of what is happening in our theatres these days. As we know, some degree of assimilation is the inevitable outcome of living within another culture: any racial group will gradually adopt many of the values and living habits of the dominant culture in order to "fit in," to become a part of that larger society. When a group attempts the opposite and tries to retain its distinct ethnic values by separating itself geographically or ideologically from the larger community, then ghettoization — physical or psychological or both — results. Rejection of assimilation (ethnocentrism) may initially appeal to some with strong racial identities, but it invariably leads to unfortunate results for all concerned: wall-building and defensiveness within an enclave, a breakdown in understanding other cultures — not just Eurocentric ones — and a resistance to those inescapable changes which all communities must undergo. Cultural isolation and violence are the usual endpoints of ethnocentric thinking.

Of course, the assimilation model has its weaknesses, too, probably the greatest being the implication that any cultural subgroup will necessarily "dilute" its unique identity by such immersion in the larger society. Is Caridad Svich, for example, an Hispanic or an American as she writes plays dealing with Cuban émigrés to our shores? Well, the fact is that she's neither and both: she's succeeded in creating a sort of hybrid identity for herself that many might find uncomfortable or confusing to deal with. And the same might be said of most of the writers in this collection. Indeed, one helpful way of understanding the field of multicultural theatre in late twentieth-century America is to regard its development as an ongoing search for new cultural identities by the ethnic groups and writers involved.

The coexistence model (with its extreme form of militant ethnocentrism) and the assimilation model have contributed much to the development of "multicultural" theatre in the 1990s; but neither seems to ring entirely true any longer in defining present trends and signaling the way ahead. Many authors like Luis Valdez may remain content writing of their own community's ethnic traditions. Others like Issac Bedonna may occasionally focus upon the social problems of one particular ethnic group in their plays. Yet there still seems to be something else going on in multicultural theatre today that is qualitatively different from either of these approaches.

Scholars Jeffrey Huberman, Brant Pope, and James Ludwig have recently argued that the United States is now the world's greatest experimental laboratory for cultural hybrids and convergences in the theatre. Richard Schechner has further defined this situation as a process of "theatrical fusion" wherein cultures mix to such a degree that a new language or genre or art form emerges. Although such terminology may sound new, it's actually based on familiar anthropological evidence drawn from theatrical history. The ancient Romans, for example, imported a great deal of Greek dramatic practice and succeeded in transforming those practices into a distinctly Latin form of theatre. More recently, the work of Bertolt Brecht, Robert Lepage, or Peter Brook has demonstrated the power of mingling intercultural elements to produce new and compelling theatrical experiences for audiences.

Something of the same sort seems to be happening today with multicultural writers here in the United States, authors who have produced a body of significant plays which are both culturally specific as well as culturally blended, and which are helping to create a new definition of mainstream American theatre. It would be inappropriate within the scope of this essay to analyze this development in great detail, but some salient features of this new "theatrical fusion" require brief mention since they'll become apparent to readers as they make their way through the pages of this collection.

Perhaps the most distinguishing feature of cultural fusion in the theatre is the new focus upon the struggle that people of color experience as they adapt to American society. Plays that celebrate the history and tradition of a specific ethnic culture (such as Migdalia Cruz's *Telling Tales*), or those that deal with poignant sociopolitical problems (like Kia Cothron's *Cage Rhythm*) are likely to continue to find their audiences in the years ahead, and some of them are represented here. But an even larger number of emerging ethnic playwrights today seem to be writing plays that focus keenly upon characters attempting to forge new identities for themselves in late twentieth-century America.

Thus, Silvia Gonzalez S. chooses the current immigration problems with Mexican undocumented workers as the backdrop for *Boxcar*, but the play's real concern is the identity crisis experienced by its Mexican-American hero — himself a border control officer — who is torn between the conflicting obligations he feels to the immigrants he interdicts and the government and people whom he represents. Similarly, Karen Huie in *Columbus Park* and *Songs of Harmony* focuses upon the rising generation of Chinese-American youth, many of whom are caught in the conflict between their parents' cultural values and the vastly different codes of accepted social behavior — sexual, religious, occupational — in contemporary America. For such writers, ethnic history or racial strife seem less important than the struggle of their characters to somehow reconcile conflicting value systems and get on with their lives in the emerging multicultural society of the United States.

A second identifiable trend in American multicultural theatre is the attempt by many playwrights to discover ways of reaching out across cultures in order to build intercultural harmony and understanding. Many writers, that is, are creating character relationships built upon cross-cultural needs and human understanding, and these plays are enjoying increasing popularity on stages across the country. Alan Brody's *Five Scenes From Life,* for example, is the story of a love affair that incongruously flowers between a white university professor and a hard-core African-American criminal within the grim walls of a penitentiary. Similarly, Berto and Marlon, two young Hispanic and Asian boys in Issac Bedonna's *Baby Jesus*, share much of their adolescence together until the play's tragic conclusion when Marlon is accidentally killed by gang violence.

A third trend in multicultural playwriting in the nineties seems to be a focus upon international culture that has only very recently emerged in multicultural plays, but which promises to attract much greater attention over the next decade as our global village continues to shrink under the influence of developing technology. Plays such as *Tokyo Carmen Versus L.A. Carmen* by Karen Tei Yamashita, or *Struggling Truths* by Peter Mellencamp are typical of this trend, where writers build upon the experience of cultural diversity here at home in order to understand the painful clash of national interests colliding upon the world stage. Whether or not ethnic playwrights here in the United States are best positioned to understand the forces of "internationalization" at work nowadays remains to be seen. What is certain, however, is that many of them are now directing their dramatic talents to this arena, and audiences are responding favorably to their efforts.

In summary, when one turns to the broad tapestry of

recent American multicultural playwriting, one is confronted by numerous crosscurrents both old and new that at first glance defy our critical understanding. Black history, an oppressive penal system, drug dealing, Cuban émigrés, illegal Mexican aliens, mixed marriages, Japanese economic competition, job discrimination — the list of dramatic subjects and ethnic sub-groups who are represented is bewilderingly long. What one can perceive, however, are a few dominant trends that seem to be emerging over the past decade and which are now creating a new American identity for all of us. But that identity is no longer "on the sidelines"; it has come to occupy center stage not just in our playhouses but also in our national life.

The sort of national identity these writers are fashioning is just as much singular and unique as it is plural and diverse; and it belongs to all of us because it reflects and challenges all of us who call ourselves Americans. If it be true that we all share the obligation today to examine and discuss what it means to be "American," then perhaps the pages of this anthology contain some helpful signposts of where we've been together and where we're heading in the years approaching the millennium and beyond. If nothing else, these writers can remind us of the common ground we share as citizens as human beings, and as co-creators in the theatrical event that happens onstage.

Multicultural Playwrights in This Anthology

Every reader of an anthology is bound to question at some point the criteria that govern the selection. With regard to this collection, some might question the ethnic "categories" of Asian/Hispanic/African-American which dictate the organiza-tion of the scenes and monologs: are the categories sufficiently inclusive? Are they too inclusive? Others may question the choice of writers: why are these included and not others? And does the book fail to make clear distinctions between writers of various subcultures within each ethnic category? Still others may find the range of material too restrictive and even reductive: does the collection say enough about where multicultural play-writing seems to be heading these days?

Firstly, readers should be aware that many cultures are cer-tainly represented in our contemporary American theatre: Arabic, Japanese, Hispanic, Native American, Caribbean, Vietnamese, and others. But the dominant strains that seem to be infusing the stage with new life today are the three presented here. African-American, Hispanic-American, and Asian-

8

American playwrights have not only succeeded in establishing a substantial body of dramatic work (one might almost say "tradition") in the American theatre, but they continue to press forward year after year with new and exciting plays that are being widely produced on stages across the country. For that reason, this anthology confines itself to those three general ethnic areas and attempts to highlight and celebrate the major artistic concerns and trends within each group.

Secondly, with regard to the particular authors selected, readers should bear in mind that this book is not designed to present only the work of the most visible and commercially successful multicultural playwrights. Instead, it emphasizes new and emerging writers whose work is not yet widely circulated in published form nor familiar to the general theatregoing public. While a few playwrights here are better known than others — Charles Smith, Migdalia Cruz, Philip Kan Gotanda — all of them have emerged as significant contributors to the American theatrical repertoire within the past decade or two and all promise new work in the years ahead.

Additionally, the book gives no special preference to male or female writers, nor to playwrights of a specific ethnic tradition, political persuasion, or artistic stamp. Some readers, for example, may feel that more Mexican authors, or more militant writers, or more avant-garde artists should have been included here. And these readers might be justified in their preferences: the growing number of anthologies devoted to particular writers testifies to the need for more critical focus upon issues of gender, politics, and race in the work of ethnic playwrights. But such considerations would be difficult to clarify in a collection of this nature.

Some plays have been included in this collection by American authors who are not of Asian, Hispanic, or African descent, or whose plays are not set in the United States. Their dramas are part of the American multicultural experience because they examine cross-cultural issues that have become very important here at home. Amlin Gray, for example, is represented here with a scene from *How I Got That Story*, a play chronicling one American journalist's encounter with southeast Asian culture during the painful years of the Vietnam War. Similarly, Peter Mellencamp's *Struggling Truths*, and Elaine Meredith Hazzard's *Seer From Saigon*, address themselves to broad cultural issues arising from the political changes that have taken place in Tibet and postwar Vietnam. And Kay Osborne's

Wipe That Smile focuses upon the situation of poor Caribbean blacks victimized by an American-dominated drug culture on the island of Jamaica.

At the same time, however, there have been some specific criteria governing the selection of scenes and monologs that readers will find in the book. Firstly, all the extracts are taken from plays produced in some form in the United States. That is, all the material has been subjected to the "litmus test" of public performance which gives playwrights the opportunity to revise and refine their works-in-progress to the point where it has become more or less "finished." Secondly, the anthology confines itself mostly to two-character or three-character scenes (and some monologs) in order to be useful for educators as resource material for readers theatre, oral interpretation, or acting classes. Finally, as a help for readers, the book concentrates on selections that contain more of a literary than a theatrical focus; and where character relationships and themes can emerge from the page more readily than ideas for innovative staging or highly experimental dramaturgy.

All the scripts contained in this anthology have been reviewed and approved by the authors, with only a minimum of editing to enable some scenes and monologs to stand free of their contexts. The brief paragraphs preceding each selection are designed to give readers helpful hints on the background of the scene and its characters, or to clarify some of the stage directions contained in the text; and the playwrights have approved these brief introductory comments as well. On occasion, a playwright has written the preface himself or herself, or has made some slight changes in the original acting version of the script especially for this anthology.

In short, this book contains excerpts from the writer's original work with only minimal editing to accommodate the needs of readers rather than those of playgoers fortunate enough to attend a production. Hopefully, readers will take away with them a heightened sense of what it means to be "American" in the late twentieth century — a sense that might give all of us some clues as to what lies on the multicultural road ahead.

NOTE: The numerals running vertically down the left margin of each page of dialog are for the convenience of the director. With these, he/she may easily direct attention to a specific passage.

SCENES AND MONOLOGS
of the Hispanic-American Experience

Baby Jesus

by Issac Bedonna

(Scene for two Hispanic men)

1   This play deals with the inspiration and hope that a poor
2   Hispanic-American family receives from a miraculous statue of
3   Christ in their home. This scene, portraying the family's sordid
4   neighborhood surroundings, is set on the rooftop of an apart-
5   ment building in a large American city. The subject is drug
6   dealing and manipulation, and the characters are lowlifes.
7   Binoculars in hand, looking downward, Elizardo explores the
8   view. He is a suave, sharp Hispanic in his twenties, a successful
9   businessman on the lookout for a new base for his drug traffick-
10   ing in the barrio. Rudy, who has brought Elizardo to the roof, is
11   in his thirties and wearing sunglasses; he's a doper and another
12   loser, but, unlike Elizardo, can be easily manipulated. As the
13   scene opens, Rudy, smoking a joint, spies something in the sky.
14

15   **ELIZARDO: Even without these, the view is excellent. Four**
16   **floors?**
17   **RUDY: Five. Look. Some "tonto" lost his birthday balloons.**
18   **ELIZARDO: This is the nineties. Probably an AIDS memorial.**
19   *(RUDY inhales smoke.)*
20   **RUDY:** *(Holding his breath)* **Yeah?** *(Exhaling)* **Ugh!** *(Beat)* **So hey,**
21   **what's up? Not everyday we get buddy-buddy on my roof.**
22   **ELIZARDO: Who said I forgave** *anyone* **– especially ten grand**
23   **worth?**
24   **RUDY:** *(Loaded)* **Loused up a deal. Well, like they say, state**
25   **your business then.**
26   **ELIZARDO: You and I are linked by a mutual need: surveil-**
27   **lance. Glad I saw this vantage point myself.**
28   **RUDY: Huh?** *(Crushing up the roach in his fingers)*
29   **ELIZARDO: Your routine up here – your setup. Your scouts.**
30   **RUDY:** *(Flicking the roach off the roof)* **Scouts? Those guys?**
31   **They live up here.**
32   **ELIZARDO: The poor illegals? No. Not the ones you rent sleep-**
33   **ing space to –** *all the comforts of a roof* **– at sky-high**
34   **prices.**
35   **RUDY: Hey, they get their own boxes to sleep in. Huh?**

1   **ELIZARDO: Your lookouts, Rudy. I'm referring to them. The**
2   **ones who keep an eye on trafficking.**
3   **RUDY:** *(Chuckling)* **Huh?** *(ELIZARDO draws closer, pointing*
4   *downstage as he speaks.)*
5   **ELIZARDO: Wonderful arrangement here. "Mira." Rose Lake**
6   **Boulevard in front of your building. Another wide road to**
7   **our right – a main artery feeding drugs into the barrio.**
8   **And, lo and behold, a grammar school, Catholic no less,**
9   **right at the corner!** *(RUDY looks down over the edge, getting*
10   *a little dizzy. He catches himself.)* **Don't fall. I won't catch**
11   **you. Don't know many people who would.**
12   **RUDY: Hey, I hear you can light a match without striking it –**
13   *(ELIZARDO holds up his hand to silence him.)*
14   **ELIZARDO: I'm not through. All those people in cars across**
15   **the street, dropping school kids off, picking them up.**
16   **Rudy's dealers, Rudy's smugglers mixing into the con-**
17   **gestion. And this is the part I'm interested in – scouts**
18   **posted on this very roof detecting in advance** *(Pointing)*
19   **any approaching police or narc. All traffickers, warned –**
20   *(He grins at RUDY who is dumbfounded at how much he*
21   *knows.)*
22   **RUDY:** *(Chuckling)* **Works like a charm!**
23   **ELIZARDO: Drug use moved way down the age range. Huh,**
24   **Rudy? No moral objections dealing to seventh and eighth**
25   **graders? Think of Snow White? "Brujas"? Poison apples?**
26   *(Mind-blown, RUDY shakes his head, chuckling.)*
27   **RUDY: "Eho le"! Can you see into the future, too?**
28   **ELIZARDO: A little bird told me –** *(Pointing to some passing*
29   *bird, trying to blow RUDY's mind)* **that one**, in fact.
30   *(Stoned, RUDY looks at the bird seriously for a moment.)*
31   **RUDY:** *(Loaded)* **Wow!**
32   **ELIZARDO: Rudy, a miraculous opportunity to be partially**
33   **forgiven.**
34   **RUDY:** *Partially? (ELIZARDO tosses the binoculars to RUDY who*
35   *catches them.)*

1 ELIZARDO: TEN GRAND UP IN SMOKE! I don't have the
2 patience of a saint. And you have a lot to redeem!
3 RUDY: Hey, I swear on a stack of Bibles —
4 ELIZARDO: I'm talking! *(Beat)* I need this rooftop for about a
5 week. I'll provide my own lookouts.
6 RUDY: Got any uppers?
7 ELIZARDO: Stop hallucinating. I'm not a drugstore.
8 RUDY: Ahh, throw in some uppers with the deal.
9 ELIZARDO: Not a chance. But — I do know, one of my look-
10 outs, constant source for grass —
11 RUDY: No lie?!
12 ELIZARDO: Thai stick.
13 RUDY: *(Quick)* Thai high?! What week do you want? Two
14 weeks?
15 ELIZARDO: Probably next week. You'll know as soon as I
16 know. *(Checking his watch)* Almost two. I'm meeting Sal
17 at his house.
18 RUDY: Bet he'll show you that old statue they got.
19 ELIZARDO: May be worth something. *(Starting to exit)*
20 RUDY: *(Chuckling)* Sal's hoping for an offer. Sweet little deal.
21 They're sweating: property taxes coming up. Leaky water
22 heater. Hey, let me ride with you to Sal's. We'll be
23 working together anyway. Huh, Elizardo? Buddy up?
24 *(ELIZARDO stops, making a clear point before they exit.)*
25 ELIZARDO: About as likely as an atheist with stigmata!
26
27
28
29
30
31
32
33
34
35

Alchemy of Desire/ Dead Man's Blues

by Caridad Svich

(Scene for two Hispanic women)

1   This lyrical, poetic play explores the nature of "desire" as it
2 traces relationships between three generations of women, one of
3 whom, Simone, has just lost her husband. The scene here is a
4 riverbank, somehow "evocative of the swamps of a burnt-out
5 bayou," where Simone is fishing. She is a passionate, restless
6 woman in her late twenties or early thirties. Miranda is a curious
7 and spirited woman in her late teens.

8

9   **MIRANDA: Ain't caught anythin yet?**

10 **SIMONE: Not yet.**

11 **MIRANDA: Gotta be patient. Gotta wait.**

12 **SIMONE: Mmmm-hmmm.**

13 **MIRANDA: I used to go fishin, so I know.**

14 **SIMONE: Yeh?** *(MIRANDA nods. Beat)*

15 **MIRANDA: Never actually fished myself, mind you.**

16 **SIMONE: Huh?**

17 **MIRANDA: My grammy'd take me. When I was little.**

18   **She's the one did the actual fishin.**

19   **I'd just watch her.** *(Pulls out a cigarette.)* **Smoke?**

20 **SIMONE: No.**

21 **MIRANDA: Yeh, she'd take me. I didn't know what was goin on.**

22   **I used to say, "Grammy, what's this? Grammy, what's that?"**

23   **"Hush, child," she'd say, "hush."** *(MIRANDA lights cigarette,*

24   *smokes.)*

25 **SIMONE:** *(To herself)* **Hush....**

26 **MIRANDA: Swear don't know how she put up with me, but**

27   **she did.**

28   **She'd just smile...sit there...fish.**

29   **She'd smoke, too.**

30   **Not cigarettes, but a big ol' cigar bout this thick.**

31   **You should've seen the smoke she'd blow out of that thing.**

32   **Swirls and swirls of it. Like chimney smoke.**

33   **And it smelled, too.**

34   **Not sweet like Caroline's perfume, but strong.**

35   **Like dust and ginger.**

1   SIMONE: Yeh?
2   MIRANDA: Used to make 'em herself, the cigars.
3   Grow the tobacco out back,
4   roll the leaves up in the finest paper —
5   suck on it till one end would be wet
6   with her saliva and juice, and then she'd light up,
7   the raw tobacco just envelopin the air.
8   Oh, and she'd smile...she'd smile the biggest grin...
9   Teeth turned black, she'd still smile.
10   I hated it. All of it. The cigars. Everythin.
11   Felt like it was a punishment every time I had to go out
12   with her. Grammy and her goddam tobacco.
13   But after awhile, I don't know how it occurred,
14   the smell of that tobacco became like heaven itself.
15   "When we goin fishin, Grammy? When we goin?"
16   "Patience, child. Patience." And she'd smile,
17   gather her gear, and take me down to the water.
18   The sun'd be comin up. You could see the rays just peerin.
19   Flashes of light bouncin off the water blindin you as you
20   looked out into the mornin haze. And she'd smile,
21   lay out the tobacco, and start rollin them cigars,
22   her hands movin sharp and quick like one of those
23   gunfighters on the TV all eyes and trigger fingers.
24   Rollin and lightin up. Smokin and castin a line.
25   It was all of a piece with Grammy.
26   I'd sit there, wallowin in the smell,
27   swear all angels had come down to pay us a visit.
28   Used to try to catch the rings of smoke with my mouth,
29   Like some sort of weird human kind of fish.
30   I must've caught a hundred rings one time. One hundred.
31   I swear, it was the best part of goin fishin.
32   'N fact, for the longest time,
33   that's what I thought fishin was:
34   just somethin you did to go smokin. *(Beat)*
35   SIMONE: Wouldn't she catch anythin?

1   MIRANDA: Every once in awhile, sure.
2   Caught a yellow perch once –
3   gutted it, chopped it up, ate it for supper.
4   But I can't say I actually remember her actually catchin
5   much of anythin in particular.
6   Not like you see in those pictures they got
7   all over the walls at the diner
8   of people standin tall next to their big fish
9   and smilin.
10   Can't say she ever got took a picture like that.
11   ...Got somethin?
12   SIMONE: Feels like somethin's on the line.
13   MIRANDA: Maybe you got somethin.
14   SIMONE: ...It's gone.
15   MIRANDA: That happens. Used to happen to Grammy all the
16   time.
17   Just when she'd think a fish bite, it'd go away.
18   They're not as stupid as we think – fish.
19   I mean, if I were a fish,
20   I wouldn't want to be somebody's supper.
21   I'd know better than to jump at the first thing I saw...
22   What you thinkin?
23   SIMONE: Hmmm?
24   MIRANDA: What you thinkin?
25   SIMONE: ...Nothin.
26   MIRANDA: Awful quiet. Gotta be thinkin bout somethin.
27   SIMONE: Just thinkin.
28   MIRANDA: What about?
29   SIMONE: ...Thinkin bout the world.
30   MIRANDA: The world? What you thinkin bout the world?
31   SIMONE: Thinkin that it's some place, y'know.
32   That it's such a big place, and all these things happen –
33   wars, fires, hurricanes, sickness –
34   I think, "How come the soil don't just *burst*?
35   How come it don't just burst from all this excitement?"

1   I know I would.

2   If it were me, I'd *explode* in a thousand little pieces,

3   scatter myself in bits all over the earth —

4   wars, fires, hurricanes comin up outta me

5   in *bile* colored gray, scarlet, and indigo.

6   Come up and out of me

7   till there'd be *nothin'*, just open space:

8   a whole other world.

9   I don't know how the soil can take it. I really don't. *(Beat)*

10 MIRANDA: Selah says the soil's stronger than all of us,

11   on account of that's where we go once we pass on.

12   ...And that's where we get our strength, too,

13   from the soil.

14 SIMONE: Yeh?

15 MIRANDA: That's what she says.

16 SIMONE: ...How you get strength from somethin that's torn

17   apart,

18   *busted* open? How you get it then?

19 MIRANDA: Maybe a different soil come up.

20 SIMONE: Huh?

21 MIRANDA: A different soil, a different earth underneath

22   the old

23   one. Maybe it'd come up and...I don't know, it'd do

24   somethin.

25 SIMONE: *(To herself)* ....Damn.

26 MIRANDA: Fish ain't jumpin for nothin, huh?

27   They'll come round.

28   Grammy'd sometimes have to wait two, three hours

29   Before a fish jump.

30   That's when she'd really put her time in smokin.

31   *(Offering another cigarette)* You sure you don't want one?

32   *(SIMONE shakes her head.)* It's good.

33 SIMONE: I know. *(Beat)*

34 MIRANDA: So, what you do, you clean the house yet?

35 SIMONE: ...No.

1   MIRANDA: Gotta clean it.
2   SIMONE: Ain't gotta *do* nothin.
3   MIRANDA: Selah says you don't clean a house after someone's –
4   SIMONE: Hell what Selah says! I ain't doin it. Ain't goin in
5   there.
6   MIRANDA: Well, she says if you don't clean it, you collect
7   bad
8   spirits.
9   And then you can't even go into the house.
10   Even if you want to.
11   Gotta *burn it down*. Cause fire's the only thing
12   that'll scare bad spirits off for good.
13   SIMONE: She say that?
14   MIRANDA: Yeh. And she said you don't get rid of bad spirits,
15   they come round and turn on you – turn you into a *spook*.
16   SIMONE: I ain't a spook.
17   MIRANDA: That's what she said.
18   SIMONE: Well, I ain't!
19   Hell, who wants to be that?
20   Nobody talkin to you, nobody lookin at you –
21   nobody wants that. *(Beat)*
22   MIRANDA: So, you gonna clean it?
23   Huh?
24   SIMONE: Gonna do somethin.
25   MIRANDA: Yeh? What you gonna do?
26   SIMONE: Gonna keep myself far away from it.
27   As far from the house as...
28   Just stay close to the water.
29   Maybe I can lose myself in it.
30   Lose myself...that'd be somethin.
31
32
33
34
35

Boxcar

by Silvia Gonzalez S.

(Scene for one Hispanic-American and
one Caucasian man)

1   This play deals with the subject of illegal aliens entering
2   the United States across the Mexican-American border. Roberto
3   is a second generation Mexican-American, in his thirties, with a
4   Boy Scout dedication to him. He and his friend Bill are border
5   patrol officers of the U.S. Immigration Service. Bill is an Anglo, a
6   regular guy, toxic at times, yet sincere. He enjoys his position as
7   a border patrol officer for the power over people it gives him. He
8   would probably be a McDonald's manager if he didn't have this
9   job. Roberto, however, is troubled by his job controlling the flood
10   of undocmented aliens. The scene is outdoors, somewhere along
11   the border. Bill is resting on the ground. Roberto writes a few
12   things on his note pad, and then reads a map.

13

14   **BILL:** *(Looks up and watches ROBERTO.)* **What are you looking**
15   **for?**
16   **ROBERT: My heritage.**
17   **BILL: Your heritage? You can't find it. No one really can. It's a**
18   **figment of the imagination. No one really cares *that far***
19   ***back.* I have no idea where I came from. Most people, I**
20   **know, don't.**
21   **ROBERT: I have an idea.**
22   **BILL: What's your last name?**
23   **ROBERT: Muñoz.**
24   **BILL: That's where your idea came from. It's only an idea.**
25   **ROBERT: A short break, Bill.**
26   **BILL: What? How about *you* snoozing a bit? Look at your eyes.**
27   **Aren't you a little bit tired? You don't sleep. That's why**
28   **you're neurotic. Sleep *is sleep.* An important element of**
29   **life.**
30   **ROBERT: I keep having these dreams. I hear voices. I see**
31   **places. I see faces that make me want to tear up.**
32   **BILL: See a therapist.**
33   **ROBERT: *This is too complicated.* No one will ever be able to**
34   **tell me anything. The answer is within me. And I'm too**
35   **freaked out to find the key. *(Pause)* Bill, what if we are**

1	doing something real wrong. I mean, look at who we are.
2	BILL: I know who I am. I'm a handsome cowboy.
3	ROBERT: I'm serious. We got to find them.
4	BILL: Well, that's our job.
5	ROBERT: But maybe we shouldn't. Maybe we should, *let*
6	*them go.* They're hiding *from us.* If they see us in the
7	forest, they go to the desert where there's no shade or
8	water. If they see us on the road, they tie themselves
9	under cars and drive by. They get killed *hiding from us.*
10	If we weren't here, Bill, travesty wouldn't fall upon them.
11	BILL: That's their problem.
12	ROBERT: Don't you *feel* anything?
13	BILL: There's a law about walking on someone's land without
14	permission.
15	ROBERT: And that's a rule that has been broken before.
16	BILL: Yeah. Like yesterday.
17	ROBERT: Like 1492.
18	BILL: Wait a minute.
19	ROBERT: And now the same rule to the newcomers.
20	BILL: Robert, you're cracked. Problems have come –
21	ROBERT: *(Overlapping from "problems")* There's always a
22	need to blame problems on the people with no voice.
23	BILL: *They've* caused problems, Robert.
24	ROBERT: When I see the face of a father with calluses on his
25	hands, I know he's here to work.
26	BILL: It's getting out of control. There are Haitians who want
27	to come in, too, but they can't. *They have no skills.*
28	ROBERT: How do you know? Did you read that in the paper,
29	or did you just guess that?
30	BILL: You are in need of sleep real bad. I suggest you get it
31	soon. Besides, this is our country and we have to take
32	care of it, or it won't be any good for anyone.
33	ROBERT: That has been said before. Since Columbus. In the
34	1500s, 1600s, all the way to the 1800s. To take care of it or
35	it won't be good anymore. Don't you see? Take care of the

1   land. Protect the land. That's what they tried to do. The
2   Indians —
3   BILL: *(Overlapping on "Indians")* **Native Americans.**
4   ROBERT: *(Continuing)* — felt a need to protect the land. They
5   were afraid that it wouldn't be good anymore if the white
6   man traversed it. They've already proved careless.
7   BILL: Yeah, so what.
8   ROBERT: And it happened. It wasn't good anymore. Less
9   hunting. The beauty, scarred, the —
10   BILL: *(Overlapping on "scarred")* I'm not going to listen to this,
11   Robert.
12   ROBERT: Roberto.
13   BILL: Since when?
14   ROBERTO: This is what I propose: *Accommodation.* Here and
15   now. Why not *cut to the chase.* Spare the ones who are
16   doing what they have to in order to survive. Hang the
17   greedy out to dry.
18   BILL: Who are the greedy?
19   ROBERTO: The ones who put up the wall.
20   BILL: When?
21   ROBERTO: After the Indians were nearly annihilated.
22   BILL: *Native Americans!*
23   ROBERTO: Don't you see, the roles are reversed. White men
24   were *the undocumented workers of that time.* Just trying
25   to fight hunger and improve their lives. Was it their fault
26   they had to take the chance of going across a land that
27   wasn't theirs? These majestic people had no concept of
28   *selling mother nature.* Let alone renting. You only bor-
29   rowed, but some white men wanted to take. So the
30   Indians *fought* to protect their borders. *They had a*
31   *border patrol.* They sent the white people *back!* But they
32   kept coming. You are proof of that. And when they
33   wouldn't stop coming, they resorted to the last possible
34   thing. War. I pity those white families, for they were only
35   looking for *a better life.* What's wrong with that? What

1   else was there to do? So they fought, probably screaming,
2   "I HAVE NOTHING TO LOSE!" And they won. Don't you
3   see, Bill? It's repeating itself. Here brown undocumented
4   workers are screaming the same thing. "I have nothing to
5   lose." And, in a slim way, they already won. *Desperate*
6   *people can win*. But at a price. They'll risk everything for
7   the sake of a better life. For their families. For their future.
8   We are preventing them to the point of killing them.
9 BILL: *COW DUNG.*
10 ROBERTO: Bill, this land always gives improvements to new-
11   comers.
12 BILL: That's it. *(Starts to exit.)*
13 ROBERTO: Come back when it's all soaked in. We'll talk
14   about what to do.
15 BILL: You know, you're —
16 ROBERTO: *(Interrupting)* Maybe I am! But so are you.
17 BILL: Why are you talking like this?
18 ROBERTO: I have Aztec *Indian* blood. It's still North American
19   Indian.
20 BILL: *Native Americans*, you dork.
21
22
23
24
25
26
27
28
29
30
31
32
33
34
35

Eddie "Mundo" Edmundo

by Lynne Alvarez

(Scene for a Hispanic man and a woman)

1   This play deals with the cultural differences experienced by
2   a young Mexican-American man, Eddie, from New York, who
3   returns briefly to his relatives' home in Nautla, Mexico. There he
4   meets the young woman, Alicia, who is betrothed to another
5   man, but who is very flirtatious. This early scene from the play
6   establishes the beginning of Eddie and Alicia's relationship. The
7   time is the 1970s, the locale is Eddie's room where he is writing
8   poetry one night.
9
10   ALICIA: Are you doing homework?
11   EDDIE: No.
12   ALICIA: Can I see what you're writing?
13   EDDIE: It's in English.
14   ALICIA: Oh.
15   EDDIE: You wouldn't understand.
16   ALICIA: Is it a poem?
17   EDDIE: Sort of.
18   ALICIA: About me – sitting here in the moonlight, pensive
19   and beautiful?
20   EDDIE: No.
21   ALICIA: Is it about your girlfriend back home with long
22   golden hair and long golden legs?
23   EDDIE: I don't have a girlfriend.
24   ALICIA: Ahhh, Edmundo the priest.
25   EDDIE: Is your boyfriend coming for you?
26   ALICIA: In a month. The next full moon.
27   EDDIE: And he'll stay away from you that long?
28   ALICIA: He didn't like it. He pleaded with me. He swore he
29   couldn't live without me. He cried. He raged like a bull.
30   He said he'd cut me or he'd die if he didn't see me soon.
31   But after all, what's a couple more weeks?
32   EDDIE: It doesn't sound like you're in love with him. You're
33   not that anxious to see him.
34   ALICIA: Well, once you're married, you know – you're
35   married! That's it.

1   EDDIE: So don't get married.
2   ALICIA: I'm not like that. Once we run away together, we'll
3   have to get married. That's the way it's done. Especially if
4   your family disapproves of the match. After you've slept
5   together – well, everyone wants you married as soon as
6   possible. The men get really mad. Machismo is nothing
7   to fool around with. Men here are very jealous.
8   EDDIE: Men there, too.
9   ALICIA: Really?
10 EDDIE: Yes.
11 ALICIA: I told my boyfriend about you.
12 EDDIE: Jesus Christ. Why?
13 ALICIA: To keep him in line.
14 EDDIE: Thanks a lot.
15 ALICIA: Can't you handle yourself?
16 EDDIE: I can handle myself and three others, if I have to.
17 ALICIA: Now you sound like one of us.
18 EDDIE: We're not so different.
19 ALICIA: Really?
20 EDDIE: Really.
21 ALICIA: Tell me – sometimes – don't you feel that when
22   someone tells you not to do something – it's the very first
23   thing you want to do?
24 EDDIE: Yeah. Sometimes.
25 ALICIA: Me, too.
26 EDDIE: Don't play with me. I don't like it. *(EDDIE continues*
27   *writing.)*
28 ALICIA: Write about me. *(EDDIE ignores her.)* You and I are
29   taking Nyin to confession tomorrow. Did Chelo tell you?
30 EDDIE: She told me.
31 ALICIA: Will you confess everything?
32 EDDIE: I have nothing to confess.
33 ALICIA: I do. Good night.
34 EDDIE: Dream of angels –
35 ALICIA: So you dream of me. Write about Pipo. Why don't you?

Latins in La-La Land

by Migdalia Cruz

(Scene for two Latinas)

1   This play, a caustic satire on the lives of the real-life
2   Menendez brothers in Los Angeles, is set both in the past and the
3   present. The two Puerto Rican sisters here, Margo and Laly, have
4   recently arrived in L.A. in 1944. They converse over old films.
5   Laly is eighteen, she desperately wants to be a Hollywood
6   musical star, and she works hard at acting assimilated. She's
7   dressed in a blue tap dance outfit, sitting on the stairs of the
8   living room with a phone nearby, waiting for her agent or a
9   director to call. She has been drinking and waiting for a long
10   time. Margo is her unambitious, but protective older sister, age
11   twenty-one, with a Spanish accent.
12
13   **LALY: Liars. Margo was right. That's why there's earthquakes**
14   **here — all the lying showbiz scumbags! I bet if they lined**
15   **up all the liars, end to end, you could reach all the way**
16   **down the earth. Past Mexico and Chile, through**
17   **Brazil...all the way to Argentina. That's what I bet. All the**
18   **way to jodida Argentina. Todo está jodido. Estamos**
19   **jodidas en jodido Hollywood.** *(MARGO is dressed in an*
20   *identical tap dance outfit, but hers is yellow. She stumbles*
21   *out and almost falls into LALY's lap.)* **Ouchie!**
22   **MARGO:** *(Semi-drunkenly, but playfully)* **Sana, sana culito de**
23   **rana. Si no sanas hoy, sanarás mañana.**
24   **LALY: Go to sleep.** *(MARGO makes a sound of disgust.)* **No?**
25   **Then eat something and stop singing about a frog's ass.**
26   **MARGO:** *(Making another sound of disgust)* **Oooey?! Why you**
27   **say such weird things?**
28   **LALY: What do you mean weird?**
29   **MARGO: Strange, mysterious, wrong-sounding —**
30   **LALY: Those are much better words than plain old weird.**
31   **What's that?! That could mean anything.** *(More gently)*
32   **Are you sure you're not hungry? I'm always hungry when**
33   **I'm hungover. It's like all the alcohol is a sauce at the**
34   **bottom of my stomach and I gotta have some bread in**
35   **there to sop it up or it'll get all rotten and then I'll feel**

1 like throwing up.

2 MARGO: Ooooey! *(Pause)* Got any sandwiches left?

3 LALY: No.

4 MARGO: Even my half esandwich de pernil?

5 LALY: You ate your half – most of it anyway. It was mostly
6 gone, and you know how fast pork goes – so in honor of
7 your health, well...tasted good too.

8 MARGO: Pig. Hog. Greedy dog. What we gonna eat?

9 LALY: We'll live on love...

10 MARGO: ¡Que pendeja!

11 LALY: *(Jokingly)* That's perfect! We could be the Pendeja
12 Sisters – like the Dolly Sisters, or the Andrew Sisters –
13 but with an edge!

14 MARGO: That's not nice – to call yourself that. I don't want to
15 be nobody's private hair anymore.

16 LALY: You wanna dance.

17 MARGO: Yes. And sing.

18 LALY: Of course. *(Pause)* But they didn't call. *(Pause)* Not this
19 time...but somebody else will. Like Papi would say, "over
20 spill-ded milk you better don' bleed."

21 MARGO: I can make my feet bleed when I dance. I got this one
22 little blister on my little toe of my left foot, and it bleeds
23 with the right kind of pressure. With the right kind of
24 pressure, it's a mess. Stockings stick so weird to you
25 when you bleed.

26 LALY: What d'ya mean weird?

27 MARGO: Weird. Strange. Unusual. Creepyish. You know –
28 weird.

29 LALY: Lupe's the best.

30 MARGO: But Dolores Del Rio has style. The dresses, the hair,
31 the lips. What's Lupe got?

32 LALY: All that – plus great comic timing. She woulda been
33 great in vaudeville –

34 MARGO: Except she's too Spanish.

35 LALY: She's not Spanish, she's Mexican.

1   MARGO: Yeah, I know, but she speaks eh-Spanishly. You
2   know what I mean. Like she never got rid of her accent.
3   Bad news when the talkies came around. You know what
4   I mean – I know you do. Don't look at me like that.
5   LALY: Like what?
6   MARGO: Like I'm estupid.
7   LALY: Sometimes you can't help what look you give people.
8   Sometimes your insides come out, showing what you
9   truly think of another person – especially one you've
10   been listening to all your life.
11   MARGO: You look at me like you'd like to kill me sometimes.
12   Do you think that's nice?
13   LALY: No.
14   MARGO: Then why do you do it?
15   LALY: Habit. Old habits are hard to –
16   MARGO: Don't say it.
17   LALY: Should we practice?
18   MARGO: No.
19   LALY: What if we forget –
20   MARGO: We won't...you might, but I'll cover for you.
21   LALY: Yeah. Right. *(Pause)*
22   MARGO: You think he's proud of us?
23   LALY: Don't know.
24   MARGO: He must be proud of us. He wouldn'ta given us the
25   money to come out here.
26   LALY: He didn't give us money – he died and we took the
27   money that he left behind. That's all. He wouldn't never
28   have given us that money if we asked him.
29   MARGO: Sure he woulda. He loves – loved us. Papi loved us.
30   LALY: Yeah...right. So much love. That's why I love those
31   Mexican movies. Dolores always looks so in love. I wanna
32   be jus' like that...
33   MARGO: I wanna take a gun and follow my man. I wanna
34   watch the sunset from the back of a horse galloping over
35   the Mexican plains. Fighting for freedom. Living for love...

1   MARGO & LALY: A Mexican spitfire.

2   LALY: Like Lupe...but the hell of it is that she always loses her

3   man to a blonde.

4   MARGO: That's why she's still popular. If she won, some-

5   body'd have something to say about it.

6   LALY: Somebody will always have something to say about

7   that, huh?

8   MARGO: It's getting chilly out here. I'm going in. Are you

9   coming?

10   LALY: Yeah. In a minute.

11   MARGO: You want a sweater? *(LALY nods "No" and MARGO*

12   *shrugs her shoulders and goes in.)*

13

14

15

16

17

18

19

20

21

22

23

24

25

26

27

28

29

30

31

32

33

34

35

Talk-Story

by Jeannie Barroga

(Scene for an Asian or Hispanic woman
and a Caucasian man)

1   This play reveals the life of Dee, a Filipina woman with a
2   penchant for emulating the heroines of forties movies, and who
3   continues her father's legacy of telling stories to herself and
4   those around her. Moving between her world of present-day San
5   Francisco and that of her father in his thirties world of rural
6   California, she tells her version of dealing with bigotry in much
7   the same way as her father told his own heroic tales to her. This
8   romantic scene takes place in a newspaper office where Dee dis-
9   cusses with her editor a feature she has just written. In the stage
10 directions for the scene, light changes distinguish between
11 moments when Dee is acting "in fantasy" or "in reality."
12
13   *(Lights indicate "reality.")*
14 **LON: We did it. Forty-five inches. Tight and clean.** *(No*
15   *response)* **Don't blend in with the woodwork, come look**
16   **at this.** *(Silence)* **If you won't be ruthless with your own**
17   **words, someone else — like me — will. I don't do well with**
18   **silent treatments.** *(DEE finally approaches.)* **Hello?**
19   **Anyone there? We speak up or it goes in like this. Is that**
20   **acceptable?** *(DEE bites her lip.)* **Okay. Good.** *(He initials it.)*
21   **Let's get this in with time to spare, and seeing as it's still**
22   **early, maybe we could, uh...** *(He glances at poster)* **if you're**
23   **not too busy, "His Girl Friday's" on...**
24 **DEE:** *(Distracted)* **You know the part about assimilation?...**
25 **LON: Dee, we've been over this...**
26 **DEE: And you took it out and I wanted it back in...**
27 **LON: And I took it out again. Dee, come on...**
28 **DEE: I want it back in.**
29 **LON:** *(Worn out)* **I see.**
30   *(Lights change to "fantasy.")*
31 **DEE:** *(Roz Russell-like)* **Lon, trying to be white, negating one's**
32   **own culture, *this* is the meat of the matter, the weighty**
33   **stuff!**
34 **LON:** *(Cary Grant-like)* **You smoke too much, and I don't mean**
35   **just cigarettes.**

1   DEE: There's safety in numbers, can't you see? Not sticking
2   out, not drawing attention to yourself...
3   LON: Like that hat. Sorry: *helmet*.
4   DEE: Lon!
5   LON: Ever wonder how many baby turkeys died for that hat?
6   DEE: I'm being serious...
7   LON: And I'm being *patient*! Dee, it's not assimilation, it's
8   sellout! The clothes, the cars, the *conveniences*! Hell,
9   they live better than me!
10   DEE: Anyone with a *broom* could live better than you! Don't
11   you ever clean this place?
12   LON: Ho, hit me where it hurts...!
13   DEE: Lon, could you focus for a moment? I'm trying to say
14   some of them will do anything to look even like *you* —
15   minus the day-old beard.
16   LON: *(Points to article.)* Dee, just don't allude to some kind of
17   takeover!
18   DEE: Assimilation does not equal takeover! God, Lon...
19   LON: Besides, you *are* like us! From what I see, you've had the
20   easiest transition of all the Asians here in America!
21   DEE: From a white perspective, of course! Who's writing this
22   article, anyway?
23   LON: *(Indicates papers.)* Okay, look at this section: your dad
24   almost got beaten up for dating a white girl. That was the
25   thirties, that doesn't apply now. There *has* been progress!
26   Awareness!
27   DEE: That's my point! There's very little progress! Why are
28   there still Asian bashings? Why is it you know nothing
29   about us? Huh? What do you know? You know Imelda,
30   you know Cory, Subic Bay, and syphilis.
31   LON: I don't know syphilis.
32   DEE: Oooooh!
33   LON: *You*'re the ones with a history of colonization. Spanish
34   *then* American! If you don't like it, change it!
35   DEE: You took the Philippines over! By some, the divine right

1   "Manifest Destiny"! They didn't want you then, and they
2   certainly don't want you now!
3   LON: No? Well, for "not assimilating," you sure blend in fast!
4   DEE: There *was* resistance, Lon! You know about the cannery
5   strikes, Watsonville, Little Manila...?
6   LON: I do now! By reading this *novel*!
7   DEE: There's a point I'm making! *(Perches on desk.)* We've yet
8   to *make our mark*! We've got to be known for more than
9   being something *not* Chinese or Japanese! For something
10   other than MacArthur, and Marcos, and the color yellow
11   and a thousand *shoes*!
12   LON: Okay! Okay! Get off the soapbox! *And* my desk!
13   DEE: Run it as it is, Lon. Take a chance. *Leave me the peep-*
14   *hole*! Give us a break. Give *me* a break. *(LON is amused.)*
15   Cut the fat here and there, but...
16   LON & DEE: ...leave the meat.
17   LON: Yes, I know! *(LON sighs, takes back paper, marks in big*
18   *letters. As he writes broadly)* Es. Tee. Eee. Tee. *Stet.*
19   Okay?
20   DEE: *(Smiles.)* Keep it. Yes.
21   *(Lights indicate "reality.")*
22   LON: *(Editing)* Good...aaah, fair...cut that..."Like a seed in a
23   tree" cut that...and that. There! Twenty inches out of
24   sixty-five, perfect. Now, if you're not busy...
25   DEE: *(Points.)* Keep this, too.
26   LON: *(Regards her.)* Okay, okay! You win. Talk about light
27   under a bushel. I couldn't get a word out of you before.
28   DEE: I wasn't sure of my issues before. I guess another "me"
29   came out.
30   LON: Well, whoever she is that was you then, I like her.
31   DEE: *(Blushes but continues.)* It's important, Lon, to have a...
32   LON: *Peephole*! *(He laughs.)* I'll never live that down! Dinner?
33   DEE: *(Taken aback)* What?
34   LON: After a movie? An oldie goldie: "His Girl Friday." Art
35   imitates life. Game?

1   **DEE: Okay. The Roxie?**
2   **LON: No.** *(Approaches her.)* **My place.**
3
4
5
6
7
8
9
10
11
12
13
14
15
16
17
18
19
20
21
22
23
24
25
26
27
28
29
30
31
32
33
34
35

Two Friends/ Dos Amigos

by Paul Morse

(Scene for one Caucasian or
African-American man, and one Hispanic))

1   This play deals with the friendship of two young boys, one
2 Anglo or African-American and the other Hispanic, who meet
3 one day playing ball. In the first two scenes they had great diffi-
4 culty communicating because neither spoke the other's
5 language, and Juan played only soccer, John only basketball
6 (John had trouble learning not to use his hands in the game).
7 John is thirteen-seventeen; Juan, the same age. The locale is an
8 outdoor basketball court on a school playground.
9   NOTE: The dialog within the markings <> indicates the
10 English translation, and is not intended to be spoken. It is
11 included here for the purpose of clarification. As the scene
12 opens, John is playing ball and Juan enters.
13
14 JUAN: Hi, John.
15 JOHN: Juan, where have you been? I haven't seen you for a
16   week.
17 JUAN: *(Broken)* I have been studying so we can speak better.
18 JOHN: English? That's great! You're doing very well.
19 JUAN: Thank you. I am inhoying it.
20 JOHN: *Enjoying* it.
21 JUAN: Oh. I am *en*joying it. Gracias.
22 JOHN: De nada. How about a game of ball?
23 JUAN: Si, ball! *(He knocks the basketball out of JOHN's hand.*
24   *JUAN dribbles very well, shoots for a basket — very*
25   *creatively — scores. JUAN turns to JOHN with a big grin.)*
26 JOHN: No.
27 JUAN: No?
28 JOHN: No, not basketball; soccer!
29 JUAN: Soccer?
30 JOHN: Si. I read a book about it. Remember the hands...
31 JUAN: Las manos?
32 JOHN: Si, las manos. No.
33 JUAN: *(Perplexed)* ¿Que?
34 JOHN: No las manos. Si.
35 JUAN: *(Remembering their encounter the week before)* ¡Ah! ¡Si,

1	no las manos! ¡Bueno!
2	JOHN: Si. Gracias. Soccer! *(He puts the ball on the ground.*
3	*Kicks it over to JUAN. JUAN returns it. They have an excel-*
4	*lent game. While the ball is in play, the following*
5	*conversation continues.)* **Oh, by the way, I talked to the**
6	**coach. He wants to meet you. I told him you were a great**
7	**ball player. And I think you'd be good on our team.**
8	JUAN: **Lo siento. No comprendo.**
9	JOHN: **I thought you were studying English.**
10	JUAN: **Si. Pero hay muchas palabras que todavia no compren-**
11	**do.** <But there are many words I still don't understand.>
12	*(The game stops. They are breathless.)* **¡Oye, eres bueno!**
13	**¡Para jugar muy bueno! Deberias de entrar a nuestro**
14	**equipo.** <Hey, you're good! Very good! You ought to join our
15	team.>
16	JOHN: **What?**
17	JUAN: **Nuestro equipo de soccer. Nuestro...** <Our soccer team.
18	Our...> *(JUAN tries to pantomime a team; he has a lot of*
19	*problems.)*
20	JOHN: **Sorry.**
21	JUAN: **Lo siento.**
22	JOHN: **Lo siento.**
23	JUAN: **Good.**
24	JOHN: **Bueno.**
25	JUAN: **Quisiera saber las palabras para decirte lo que quiero**
26	**decirte. Eres bueno para jugar soccer. Serias un ben**
27	**jugador para nuestro equipo de soccer. ¿Como podria**
28	**decirte lo que quiero que sepas? ¡Ah! Se me olvidaba...** <I
29	wish I knew the words to tell you what I want to tell you.
30	You're good. You'd be an asset to our soccer team. How can
31	I tell you what I want you to hear? Ah! I almost forgot...>
32	*(Slowly)* **Yo tengo un libro para usted.** *(He takes the book*
33	*out of his back pocket.)*
34	JOHN: **A book?**
35	JUAN: **Si. I have a vook for you.**

1   JOHN: *Book.*

2   JUAN: *Book.* *(Corrects himself.)* **I have a book for you.**

3   JOHN: *(Crossing to him, looking)* **What book?**

4   JUAN: **"Say it in Spanish." Español para Ingles.** <Spanish for

5   English.>

6   JOHN: **Gee, that's great, Juan. But why would I want to speak**

7   **to you in Spanish?**

8   JUAN: **So we can speak to each other better.** *(Testing himself)*

9   **Para que nos hablemos mejor. Si.** <So we can speak to each

10   other better. Yes.>

11   JOHN: **But why would I want to learn Spanish? You're learn-**

12   **ing English.**

13   JUAN: **No comprendo.**

14   JOHN: **I don't understand. Why should I speak Spanish, I live**

15   **in America. We speak English here.**

16   JUAN: *Tu* **hablas Ingles.** *You* **speak English. There are many**

17   **here that speak Spanish. And many here who speak**

18   **Chinese. And Indian and French, and German. America**

19   **is a home for everyone. And everyone should be able to**

20   **speak to everyone.**

21   JOHN: **That's why they should learn English!**

22   JUAN: **Pensaras que todo vino de America. You must think**

23   **everything came** *from* **America. Pero hay muchas cosas**

24   **que vinieron a America. But there are many things that**

25   **came** *to* **America. Like...tacos. ¿Te gustan los tacos?** *(JOHN*

26   *shrugs.)* **Do you like tacos?**

27   JOHN: **Sure, they're good. Sure, I like tacos?**

28   JUAN: **Where do you think they came from? McDonald's?**

29   JOHN: **Taco Bell.**

30   JUAN: **Taco Bell? No, Mexico! And the guitar!** *(JOHN pan-*

31   *tomimes playing a rock song.)* **La guitarra vino de España.**

32   **The guitar came from Spain. And also the name Los**

33   **An<j>eles. It's Spanish. So you already** *speak* **Spanish.**

34   JOHN: **But we pronounce it Los An<g>eles.**

35   JUAN: *(JOHN hands the book back to JUAN. He doesn't take it.)* **I**

1   have lived in America for only a few months. My family
2   heard a lot about America in Mexico. The golden land,
3   they told us. That there were lots of opportunity for my
4   folks here. And America is indeed a golden land. But
5   there is also a lot of intolerance here. The Spanish have
6   a very rich history. We are *so* close, but who here in
7   America knows a little of our history? Our culture? Our
8   heroes? We know about Lincoln, and Kennedy, and
9   Disneyland. But what do you know about Juarez, Pancho
10   Villa, or the Panda Bears? *(Slight pause. JOHN stands*
11   *humbled.)* You and I. We can have fun. But we can also be
12   friends. If we are to do that then we must be able to talk
13   to each other. Or else, there will be nothing for us to talk
14   about. Good-bye, John. See you around. *(JUAN exits.)*
15
16
17
18
19
20
21
22
23
24
25
26
27
28
29
30
31
32
33
34
35

Alchemy of Desire/ Dead Man's Blues

by Caridad Svich

(Monolog for a Hispanic woman)

1   This lyrical, poetic play explores the nature of "desire," of

2   the power of love to endure beyond death. It traces relationships

3   between three generations of women, one of whom, Simone, has

4   just lost her husband, Jamie, and is trying to deal with her grief.

5   She is a passionate, restless woman in her late twenties or early

6   thirties. Here, following the death of her husband, she speaks of

7   her empty life and empty home, and her desire to escape her feel-

8   ings by just "going fishing." The earlier scene in this section

9   between Simone and Miranda followed directly upon this

10   monolog.

11

12   **Truth is, I married him.**

13   **When you come right down to it,**

14   **I'm the one who did the marryin.**

15   **Jamie just fell into it.**

16   **n fact, I'd say we sort of fell into each other:**

17   **He didn't know what he was doin,**

18   **and I was still burnin with the memory**

19   **of havin made love in his car.**

20

21   **It's a strange thing: desire.**

22   **It makes you do things for no other reason**

23   **than a mighty feelin you can't even put your finger on**

24   **says you *got* to do it.**

25   **...Strange.**

26

27   **Haven't cleaned up the house yet.**

28   **Haven't even been in the house,**

29   **not for more than an hour or two at a time, not since the wake.**

30   **I don't wanna go in there.**

31   **It still smells like fried chicken.**

32   **n what stuff he had is in there, too.**

33   **s too pitiful to sit around, touch it...wouldn't know what to do.**

34

35   **I sleep in the yard.**

1   It's been so hot,
2   the cool nights feel good against my skin.
3   I like being next to the earth, right up against it,
4   lettin the moss tickle my belly n my toes,
5   have it lick at my feet like a strange animal.
6   Feels good sinkin into the moist earth unencumbered.
7   Gives a sense of peace to things,
8   kind of peace can't feel nowhere else.
9
10   Some nights I pretend I'm dead:
11   that I'm just a body
12   restin on a piece of burial ground somewhere,
13   waitin for the heavens to take my soul away —
14   like those bodies you see lyin about sometimes,
15   people you ain't never met, never seen even,
16   forgotten bodies that somehow are at peace on the ground
17   indebted to the cruelty of nature — that's what I pretend.
18   It's gotten to where I can hold my breath for a minute
19   ...sometimes two.
20
21   I lie on the cool ground, motion-less
22   holdin my breath —
23   *(To herself)* **Hush** —
24   in hope that no one will find me,
25   that I will simply be lost forever,
26   gone from this world....
27
28   But then a sound or a light in the sky will stir me,
29   and I am no longer at rest on a burial ground
30   but lyin all too awake in my yard,
31   sleepless, stirrin,
32   eyes that had been dreamless suddenly wide in motion,
33   searchin for the first signs of light.
34
35   I stay there. Eyes open. Starin at nothingness.

1   Until, sure enough, I see the hard sparkle of the sun
2   hit the edge of the fence,
3   bounce against Lucy Hawkins' windowpane
4   and cut across my eyelids – close, hot.
5
6   I get up. I go into the house. I take off my clothes.
7   I pour myself a tall, very tall, glass of mint julep ice tea
8   with much too much ice, and when I finish the glass
9   just as it is beginning to cool itself right through me –
10 the stench, the wretched stench of the chicken,
11 and of the candy-sweet perfumes
12 Caroline and Selah wore that day,
13 sends me back outside:
14 where I throw on an old dress
15 that's been hangin on the line too long
16 over my body,
17 and take off
18 down to the water.
19 Down to the water...and go fishin.
20
21
22
23
24
25
26
27
28
29
30
31
32
33
34
35

Graffiti

by Nilo Cruz

(Scene for a Hispanic-American man and woman)

1   Lucy is a young, spirited woman in her twenties, and
2   Bruno is a young man in his late twenties or early thirties.
3   Underneath the domestic concerns they share in the scene with
4   Lucy's twelve-year-old brother, there is a strong, sensitive subtext
5   of love and mutual respect that develops between them. The
6   place is Lucy's small apartment in New York's inner city. The
7   time is the present.

8

9   **LUCY:** *(Offstage)* **He's running loose again. I told him next**
10   **time I'm not getting him out. Maybe you can tell him**
11   **something. He doesn't listen to me.**
12   **BRUNO: That kid is hardheaded.**
13   **LUCY: He won't tell me who he was with, 'cause no one else**
14   **got caught but him. He's got bad luck.** *(She enters with*
15   *shoes in her hand.)*
16   **BRUNO: I heard you don't like anybody coming here.**
17   **LUCY: Who told you that?**
18   **BRUNO: Your brother.**
19   **LUCY: Not you. You're always welcome here. I did tell Waldo I**
20   **didn't want him bringing his friends...I don't want those**
21   **kids in here. They break things in the house. Not that I**
22   **have anything valuable. I just don't want them here.**
23   **They don't respect their own mothers. Don't want kids**
24   **like that in my house. Let me dry the floor.** *(Takes a mop.)*
25   **I was cleaning before you came.**
26   **BRUNO: Who lives downstairs?**
27   **LUCY: The owner. She's a real nice Polish woman.**
28   **BRUNO: Pay a lot?**
29   **LUCY: Wouldn't be able to live here if it was a lot of rent. It's**
30   **not bad for four walls. In most places they don't let you**
31   **have animals. The owner lets Waldo have his cat. He's got**
32   **four now. Booboo just gave birth to four kittens. But she**
33   **won't let anybody near them, except Waldo. That's her**
34   **box there.**
35   **BRUNO: Where are the kittens?**

1   LUCY: I can never tell where she hides them. She had her
2   kittens underneath our bed and she moved them. She
3   placed them underneath the cupboard. Then she moved
4   them again. Booboo's always looking for a new place for
5   them. I like seeing how she drags her kittens by the skin
6   of their necks. Never stays in one place for too long.
7   BRUNO: She's a street cat.
8   LUCY: She sure is. Waldo found her somewhere. Would you
9   like some lemonade?
10   BRUNO: Sure.
11   LUCY: *(Goes to get lemonade.)* I tell Waldo, that cat reminds
12   me of Mami. She was always trying to find a better place
13   for us. She was always moving us by the skin of our
14   necks, 'cause her hands were too full with other things.
15   We went from one place to another. We moved to one
16   neighborhood because it was cheaper, to another
17   because it was safer. Until we ended back here. The same
18   place from where we started from. My mom was like a
19   street cat.
20   BRUNO: I can say the same for myself. I'm always trying to
21   find a better place to be.
22   LUCY: That's the way it is. *(She feels the table with her hand.)*
23   This table needs oiling. I'll get something to oil it with.
24   BRUNO: Why don't you just sit down and relax.
25   LUCY: You're right. *(Smiles.)* I feel like I never stop. There's
26   always something to do. The wood gets dry from cleaning
27   it with a wet rag. It gets old and brittle.
28   BRUNO: Do I make you nervous?
29   LUCY: No, it's not you.
30   BRUNO: Then be still for a while.
31   LUCY: I'm sorry.
32   BRUNO: *(Holds her hand.)* There's nothing to be sorry about.
33   LUCY: *(Moves her hand.)* It just feels that way sometimes, like
34   I never stop. Tomorrow I don't work out there but I work
35   here. I help the owner clean her place. She's old and

1   needs help. Then I come here and do my stuff.
2   BRUNO: Everything looks clean to me.
3   LUCY: It's all dusty in here. Dust gets everywhere.
4   BRUNO: I don't see it.
5   LUCY: That's because you don't live here.
6   BRUNO: You know what an old friend of my father's used to
7   say about having a woman in the house?
8   LUCY: What?
9   BRUNO: He said it was like having a ripe fruit, a ripe guava.
10   LUCY: Why a guava?
11   BRUNO: Because when guavas are ripe they make the whole
12   house smell. They make the house smell inviting, like a
13   fruit.
14   LUCY: Really.
15   BRUNO: It's true. I can smell it here.
16   LUCY: Does it smell like guava?
17   BRUNO: *(Holds her hand.)* It does. *(They look at each other.)* You
18   work too much. I'd like to take you out. I'd like to take
19   you out somewhere where we could dance and enjoy our-
20   selves. Do you ever go out?
21   LUCY: I do.
22   BRUNO: Where?
23   LUCY: I go out.
24   BRUNO: You're lying.
25   LUCY: I do go out.
26   BRUNO: Where?
27   LUCY: I go out. Except I don't go out to any particular place.
28   Sometimes I take the public bus and I go somewhere.
29   BRUNO: And where is that?
30   LUCY: Wherever it takes me. I just go somewhere. I take the
31   bus and ride it. I like doing that. I figure that all buses
32   have a route. They go somewhere, then they come back.
33   And I just want to go somewhere. Want to be taken some-
34   where. I don't care where. Don't want to think of a place
35   to go. I just want to go. I want to distract myself looking

1   at the streets, the people, the stores. Haven't you ever felt
2   like doing that? Just to be taken somewhere, anywhere.
3   I'd go to the moon if I could. Get tired of these four walls,
4   and I want to see something different. I learn by watch-
5   ing people, looking at a tree. I learn about myself. Would
6   you like some more lemonade?
7   BRUNO: Sure.
8   LUCY: *(Goes for the pitcher.)* I'm going to cook dinner when
9   Waldo gets home. Would you stay?
10   BRUNO: Sure.
11   LUCY: *(Brings pitcher and another glass.)* I'm glad you get
12   along with my brother.
13   BRUNO: He's a good kid.
14   LUCY: I worry about him.
15   BRUNO: Why?
16   LUCY: I don't know where he's at sometimes. I don't know
17   where he goes. I'm concerned about what kind of friends
18   he has. I feel I'm responsible for him. When my mother
19   died, I felt she put him in my hands to take care of him.
20   And I feel I have to do so. I have to set a good example for
21   him. He's got no one to do that but me.
22   BRUNO: But he's not a kid.
23   LUCY: I know. But he needs guidance. He needs to know he
24   has a home. Things are bad as they are. They've been bad
25   enough for a while with Papi turning his back on us. A
26   boy like Waldo needs authority, the guidance of a father.
27   He doesn't listen to me. And he's beginning to like the
28   streets too much. This is the second time I've had to pick
29   him up at the police station for writing on a wall.
30   BRUNO: Most kids do that.
31   LUCY: I know, but it's against the law. It's vandalism. It's
32   wrong. Why do that? Why mess up the place where we
33   live? Look at our streets. They're filthy. Is it because we
34   hate ourselves? Each other? Is it because we hate where
35   we live? Our neighborhood is poor. This house is falling

1	apart. But I keep a clean house and that's what matters.
2	Decency is what counts. The rich don't mess up their
3	walls. Their neighborhoods are clean, their streets.
4	BRUNO: I know what you're saying. But I don't know about
5	the hate stuff. I don't hate you.
6	LUCY: I know you don't. I didn't mean it that way. I just think
7	about these things when I walk the streets and I look
8	around me. If we cared for ourselves we wouldn't destroy
9	the place where we live. We wouldn't harm each other.
10	We kill each other – you can read it in the paper every
11	day. You can read the headlines. *(Pause)* The other day I
12	ate Chinese food at work. We do that sometimes. We
13	order food from the Chinese restaurant across the street.
14	And after I ate, I got my fortune cookie and opened it.
15	Inside it had two fortunes. I was surprised to get two
16	instead of one. One said, "A friend is a present you give
17	yourself," or something like that. The other one said...
18	*(Pause)* ...it went like this: "Society prepares the crime,
19	the criminal commits it." And I thought to myself, that's
20	what we are. We are criminals. The crime is prepared for
21	us, and we commit it – we get up in the morning to
22	commit the crime. We go to work to commit the crime –
23	I know I'm not explaining myself. But it is clear to me
24	sometimes. It's the system of our country. Some of us are
25	trained in the art of the crime and some of us aren't. You
26	can go to school to learn to be good at it. The rest of us
27	just learn to nip and slash and leave a mess behind
28	us...When I tell Waldo these things, he doesn't under-
29	stand. He just says I'm not cool. *(Laughs.)* But I can tell
30	when he's cool. I can tell when he's been out there scrib-
31	bling. I can tell by his hands. I tell him all that paint on
32	his hands is going to kill him. I scare him. I tell him it's
33	poisonous and it's going to get into his skin, his veins,
34	and kill him.
35	BRUNO: *(Laughs.)* You're kidding!

1 LUCY: It's true. All that dye gets into your system and kills you.

2 BRUNO: He'll grow out of it.

3 LUCY: He's better now that you've become his friend. He

4   respects you. He looks up to you. And it's good for him to

5   have a friend older than he is.

6 BRUNO: And you, Lucy?

7 LUCY: What? You want to know if I respect you?

8 BRUNO: Well, if you put it that way...can we break the respect

9   and be disrespectful? *(Kisses her on the lips.)*

10

11

12

13

14

15

16

17

18

19

20

21

22

23

24

25

26

27

28

29

30

31

32

33

34

35

Telling Tales

by Migdalia Cruz

(Monolog for a Latina)

1   This collection of monologs describes the experiences of
2   Puerto Rican women who grew up in the South Bronx. Mixtures
3   of childhood memories, family experiences, and present-day
4   outlooks, each of the stories creates an unforgettable, unique,
5   and detailed image of these women's reflections on their lives.
6   The following monolog, "Rats," centers upon one character's
7   (the women are not given names) struggle to come to terms with
8   and control her past and not be driven or dominated by it.
9

10   He says violence is not the answer. They're just looking
11   for a warm place to live out the winter, and in the spring
12   they'll be gone. But I hear them. In the walls. In the drawers.
13   Every day I check the flour for them. They get everywhere. He
14   says we shouldn't kill them. That won't keep them from
15   coming back. He's a scientist, so he knows. He also says how
16   can you kill anything that's so cute.
17   "But they ate all my sweet corn and my marigolds and my
18   squash seeds," I say. "We can buy more," he says. I say, "Why
19   should we have to?" I say, "They're aliens, invaders. Get the
20   hell out of my seeds and grains." I'm not a monster. I'm
21   willing to give them my thyme. It's all dried up now anyway,
22   but there's plenty of it. And it's right there in the front yard.
23   Right where they can get their grimy little teeth on it. But no.
24   They gotta come inside my house.
25   I never liked mice. The ones in my parents' apartment
26   were gray — baby rats, really. Nobody cared about the souls of
27   those guys. They were dirty, ugly and smelled like urine, other
28   animals' urine — not even their own urine, you know what I
29   mean? City mice are nobody's friends. You kill city mice. You
30   don't gently catch them in Hav-A-Heart traps and release them
31   into some pretty country field. There are no fields, so if you let
32   'em go they will (a) come back, or (b) bite you and give you
33   rabies. So you have no choice. You use those lovely, back-
34   breaking snap traps. By doing this, you prevent disease,
35   death, desolation. You keep little rats from becoming big rats

1   that will eat small children.

2   My father caught rats at work. They had contests to see
3   who could catch the biggest one. The danger, of course, was
4   that the rat might break out of the plastic bag it was caught in
5   and rush the crowd of laughing men, throwing down their
6   dollar bills in drunken bets. The rats usually lost.

7   There was this one guy – Paco Loco – my dad says
8   Dominicans will do anything for money – who was offered
9   twenty dollars to catch a rat with his bare hands and strangle
10   it. Paco went after a big one, but he slipped when he got right
11   up to it and had cornered it. As he grabbed for it, the rat
12   jumped smack into his face, bit him and kept running past the
13   other men who all ran screaming out the door. My dad was the
14   only one who stayed. He says the rat stopped and looked at
15   him. He said it looked scared. Imagine that. Even with blood
16   hanging off his teeth, he was still scared of people. Then he
17   kept right on going, under the steel machinery, disappearing
18   into the wall. My dad went over to Paco and helped him up.
19   Paco was crying. The rat got his left eye. I mean, it was com-
20   pletely gone. It was just a hole.

21   They stopped playing with the rats after that.

22   I thought I left those things behind me. In the Bronx. But
23   they followed me here. To white suburbia. I'm the only Puerto
24   Rican in New Canaan, Connecticut. I figure as long as I don't
25   open my mouth I'm safe. I was at a party once and some
26   WASPy lady in tennis whites asked if I was from England.
27   England?! Can you imagine?! She said she thought I was from
28   England because I had an accent. She looked real surprised
29   when I told her I was from the South Bronx. "South what?"
30   But once she got used to the idea, it seemed quite wonderful
31   and she grabbed my elbow and brought me around to all of
32   her friends. "Have you met this wonderful creature yet? She's
33   from the Bronx – the South Bronx!" "Amazing! Is anybody
34   still living there?" No – nobody important...just people. My
35   mother, my father, my sisters. The priest who gave me first

1   communion. My friend Sharon whose little brother Junie
2   died of sickle cell anemia when we were twelve and he was
3   ten. She's a cop now. I bet she's a good cop. Forty-fourth
4   precinct. Otherwise known as Fort Apache. It's funny...when I
5   lived there it seemed like Fort Navajo or Fort Chippewa. My
6   people are a peaceful people. It's when they herd us into
7   *barrios* that we turn – like a rat in a plastic bag. When you're
8   fighting for your life you get ugly. You get bitter. Or if you're
9   like my mother, you spend a lot of time in church lighting
10 candles. And you bring your children with you so they forget
11 for a time that they've been forsaken.
12   The church is beautiful. It smells wonderful. It smells
13 purple, like a purple, powerful drug. I loved the church. When
14 I was sixteen I decided to become a part of the church. You
15 know, settle down, get married to the Son of God. But it didn't
16 work out too well. I liked to read too much. And I liked to
17 write. Mother Superiors don't like that kind of stuff. After
18 three weeks, four days, nine hours, I left. I think my mom was
19 disappointed. Back to the Bronx. Wasn't any one of us going
20 to get out? The Bronx – where people talk with such intrigu-
21 ing accents.
22   He doesn't understand why they upset me so much. With
23 their cute little noses and big, brown eyes. They look just like
24 his eyes. Just like mine. But they squeak. I don't squeak, do I?
25 Maybe I do. Maybe I shouldn't be afraid of them, but I am. The
26 scuttling sounds behind the wall remind me. I wonder if what
27 they say is true – that you have the memories of all your
28 ancestors inside your head. I wonder if my children will jump
29 when they hear mice in the walls. I wonder if they'll remem-
30 ber too and get up in the middle of the night to check on
31 people who aren't there anymore....
32   Maybe he's right. Maybe it's time to put away the knife.
33
34
35

Gleaning/Rebusca

by Caridad Svich

(Scene for two Hispanic-American women)

1   This play examines the lives of Cuban-Americans living in
2 southern Florida. Sonia and Barbara are close friends and have
3 been sharing an apartment for some time. Both have been
4 seeking marriage, but it is Barbara who receives a proposal from
5 a young man named Orlando. In this scene the two women
6 discuss preparations for the wedding, and the way in which
7 Barbara's marriage will change their relationship. Underneath
8 the surface of their conversation, however, we begin to suspect
9 that Barbara is not entirely comfortable about marrying
10 Orlando, perhaps because of her relationship to another man
11 named Rudy. We also suspect that Sonia's happiness for her
12 friend's wedding only partially reflects the emotions she truly
13 feels. As the scene opens, Barbara is sorting through makeup in
14 a box and Sonia is clipping items from a shopping catalog.
15
16 **SONIA: So, it's official?**
17 **BARBARA: We're engaged.** *(Slight pause)* **That's it.**
18 **SONIA: That's something.**
19 **BARBARA:** *(After a pause)* **Until we have a ring...**
20 **SONIA: Gotta have a ring.**
21 **BARBARA: Or else what's the point?** *(Slight pause)* **I think it'll**
22   **be good. Don't you?**
23 **SONIA: At least you'll have something.**
24 **BARBARA: It'll be good.**
25 **SONIA:** *(After a pause)* **He loves you.**
26 **BARBARA: I can't wait to marry him.**
27 **SONIA: Then what?**
28 **BARBARA: Then we'll be together.**
29 **SONIA:** *(After a pause)* **You could live with him.**
30 **BARBARA: No. I want a wedding. I want it to be permanent.**
31   **It's the only way.**
32 **SONIA: I'll be lucky if I see you.**
33 **BARBARA: Huh?**
34 **SONIA: Nothing.** *(Slight pause)* **You've thought about the dress?**
35 **BARBARA: I don't have a ring yet.**

1   SONIA: The tailors around here are super busy. You go
2   waiting around taking your time and –
3   BARBARA: I'll make an appointment.
4   SONIA: You better make it soon.
5   BARBARA: I'll make an appointment.
6   SONIA: If you don't make it soon –
7   BARBARA: Sonia!
8   SONIA: *(After a pause)* I haven't said a word.
9   BARBARA: I told you I'd do it.
10   SONIA: If you mess up, you mess up.
11   BARBARA: *(To herself)* And you keep on and on.
12   SONIA: If it's a disaster, it's a disaster. It's not my business.
13   *(Slight pause)* You gonna do pink or white? Don't tell me
14   one of those strange colors like peach or blue *que va* a
15   look like *los carnavales.*
16   BARBARA: White. I'll do white.
17   SONIA: *(After a pause)* Babi, Orlando's a treasure. Thinking
18   about Rudy won't help.
19   BARBARA: I'm not.
20   SONIA: Your eyes are doing something.
21   BARBARA: I'm thinking.
22   SONIA: About Rudy.
23   BARBARA: Just thinking. What are you, wound up today?
24   SONIA: *(After a pause)* Every time I say something...
25   BARBARA: It's too much! The engagement, the wedding, this,
26   that. I don't have time to pee and now I have to think
27   about these things? It's too much.
28   SONIA: *(After a pause)* Ay!
29   BARBARA: What?
30   SONIA: A fly.
31   BARBARA: Where is it?
32   SONIA: Flew away. *Una picazón.*
33   BARBARA: Don't scratch.
34   SONIA: It itches.
35   BARBARA: That's what they want. Damn flies want you to

1   scratch, scratch, scratch till it swells up like a bowling
2   ball. I'll get the Caladryl.
3 SONIA: I'm all right.
4 BARBARA: It's the best thing.
5 SONIA: I won't scratch.
6 BARBARA: Well, remind me to put some on you later. 'Cause
7   if not...
8 SONIA: I know.
9 BARBARA: *(After a pause)* I wonder who'll come to visit?
10   Didn't your mami used to tell you that? When a fly comes
11   in, that means someone will come to visit?
12 SONIA: No.
13 BARBARA: Mine did. Whenever a fly would come in, I'd
14   spend the next day or two waiting. Somebody always
15   showed up.
16 SONIA: Really?
17 BARBARA: Without fail.
18 SONIA: *(After a pause)* Sometimes I think no one's going to
19   come along.
20 BARBARA: You got Polo.
21 SONIA: Yeah, he's intense, but I'm talking about someone. I'll
22   see him, he'll see me, and I know he'll be someone. With
23   Polo, I still feel like I'm waiting.
24 BARBARA: You don't see each other enough.
25 SONIA: We see each other plenty. But when we're in bed
26   together, it's like it's just me, me and what I'm thinking.
27   *(Slight pause)* We could be so good we could be great.
28 BARBARA: There are other guys.
29 SONIA: I want to work it out with him. You worked it out with
30   Orlando.
31 BARBARA: We're engaged.
32 SONIA: Exactly. You're going somewhere.
33 BARBARA: *(After a pause)* Doesn't hurt to look.
34 SONIA: If I look, I'll start touching.
35 BARBARA: So?

70

1   **SONIA:** So what would Polo think?
2   **BARBARA:** *(Selects lipstick from the box.)* **He'll think you're hot.**
3   **SONIA:** Yeah?
4   **BARBARA:** *Candela.* *(BARBARA puts on lipstick. SONIA*
5   *watches her.)*
6
7
8
9
10
11
12
13
14
15
16
17
18
19
20
21
22
23
24
25
26
27
28
29
30
31
32
33
34
35

The Migrant Farmworker's Son

by Silvia Gonzalez S.

(Scene for two Hispanic-American men)

1   This play portrays the struggle of a poor Mexican-American
2   immigrant family to adapt to the different social customs of
3   modern American society. Centering largely upon the conflict
4   between young Henry, who is fast becoming "Americanized,"
5   and his father, who longs to return to Mexico, it highlights many
6   of the conflicts such families experience who find themselves
7   torn between the cultural values of their homeland and the new
8   value systems of their adopted nation. In the following scene,
9   the conflict between teenage Henry and his father reaches a dan-
10   gerous climax as the father tries to assert his authority.
11   Throughout the drama, the playwright uses a group of silent
12   Mexican peasants with blue skin and gray-blue clothing to move
13   in and around the action, like the *kyogen* of the Oriental theatre,
14   supplying properties, changing scenes, etc. The setting is the
15   kitchen of the family's home in Yuma, Arizona. As the scene
16   opens, Henry is at the kitchen table doing his homework when
17   his father enters and stands there, staring at Henry.
18
19   **HENRY: Dad, I have homework to do.** *(No response. Still more*
20   *staring)* **Dad, leave me alone. I'm doing** *tarea.*
21   **DAD: Tarea. ¡Digalo bien!**
22   **HENRY: Tengo ser me tarea.** *Adesso.*
23   **DAD: Adesso? Eso es Italiano.**
24   **HENRY: I like Italian. And for your information, that's where**
25   **I'll go if I'm going to travel.** *There,* **or Egypt. See, I already**
26   **know about Mexico.**
27   **DAD: No, you don't. I thought I knew everything about the**
28   **United States, and when I came here, I was mistaken.**
29   **Where's your mother?**
30   **HENRY: She went to class.**
31   **DAD: I told her not to go.**
32   **HENRY: Give her a break.**
33   **DAD: She's planning to leave me.** *(Long pause)* **In this house,**
34   **vamos hablar puro Español, des de ahora.**
35   **HENRY: Speak in Spanish only? Not on your life.**

1 DAD: You're going to write your homework in Spanish. And if
2 you don't, out you go.
3 HENRY: I'll go! *(HENRY gets up, but DAD grabs him and throws*
4 *him into the chair.)* I'll fail if I write this in Spanish.
5 DAD: I failed, too! Comiensa su tarea en español.
6 HENRY: Dad!
7 DAD: ¡En este momento! ¡Andale! *(DAD pushes HENRY off the*
8 *chair.)*
9 HENRY: Go to hell! *(DAD pulls out his belt. A blue Mexican*
10 *peasant appears. He is holding a belt and watching the*
11 *action.)*
12 DAD: Venga aqui. Lloron. You baby.
13 HENRY: Baby? I saw you near the canal crying. Crying! You
14 are a grown man who cries near the canal! Macho,
15 macho, macho.
16 DAD: I'm going to kill you.
17 HENRY: Go ahead and do it! It just doesn't hurt me anymore!
18 DAD: If your mother could hear you talking to me in this way.
19 HENRY: If I told her you never stopped, she'd leave you! And
20 you would be *solo! Muy solo!*
21 DAD: So you think I'm an animal?
22 HENRY: No, Dad, I think *you're crazy*. *(DAD is about to strike*
23 *HENRY, but HENRY protects himself by picking up a basket*
24 *of laundry and throwing it towards DAD.)*
25 DAD: You run from su papa, and I'll beat you harder.
26 HENRY: ¡Tu no eres mi papa!
27 DAD: Venga aqui.
28 HENRY: No. You're going to hit me.
29 DAD: I'll hit you harder if you don't come *en este momento*.
30 HENRY: You'll hit me anyway. *(DAD stares at HENRY for a long*
31 *time. HENRY weakens to his DAD's authority. He then*
32 *approaches DAD, stops, and turns around to get hit.)*
33 DAD: I'll kill you.
34 HENRY: Go ahead. Being dead is better than this.
35 DAD: En Español.

1   **HENRY:** No. *(DAD raises the belt and at the top, freezes. The*
2   *blue Mexican peasants start swinging belts in slow motion*
3   *during HENRY's monolog. HENRY will be stoic as he*
4   *speaks, staring straight out.)*
5   **HENRY:** See, Dad, it was bound to happen. I got used to it. I
6   got used to all the beatings. Ever wonder if that would
7   happen? This is not how you get respect. If only I had
8   brothers and sisters to share in this delightful activity. If
9   only they'd been here to either take it with me, or help
10   me in telling you how wrong you are in doing this. Ever
11   since I was little I had to cover what you did to me. I had
12   to have a smile on my face and pretend nothing hap-
13   pened. So no one would suspect. Never see my shame.
14   Never let anyone know what happens in this house. Keep
15   hitting me, Dad, if it makes you feel better. After all, this
16   is your house. I am a snake in the grass for not under-
17   standing you. For being too young and stupid to know
18   why you hurt. I will always remember the beatings with
19   pity for you, because the scars of this will be a lot deeper
20   for you.
21
22
23
24
25
26
27
28
29
30
31
32
33
34
35

SCENES AND MONOLOGS

of the African-American Experience

Wipe That Smile

by Kay M. Osborne

(Scene for an African-American man and woman)

1   Putus and Phanso struggle to make a decent life for them-
2   selves and their children in Jamaica, despite the way they're
3   exploited by other Blacks — like Putus' employer Miss Scarlett —
4   who traffic in drugs, by the business interests who control the
5   island's economy, and by so many others who are all "on the
6   make." Beneath the marital bickering of this comic scene,
7   however, there is an authenticity to their lives; and the deep love
8   and mutual respect they hold for each other defies any simple
9   stereotyping of these characters. Phanso is unemployed, about
10 twenty-six years-old; Putus is his common law wife, about his
11 same age, and mother of his two children. The locale is Miss
12 Scarlett's swanky Kingston apartment where Putus works as a
13 live-in maid.
14
15 PUTUS: *(Humming and singing)* **The Lord's my shepherd, I'll**
16   **not want. He makes me down to lie. In pastures green, he**
17   **leadeth me, the quiet waters by...My soul he doth,**
18   **restores to life. An' me to walk doth make...** *(She hears a*
19   *soft knock at the door. PUTUS walks through the living*
20   *room to the door while drying her hands on her skirt.)*
21   **Who's that?**
22 PHANSO: *(Offstage)* **Phanso.**
23 PUTUS: *(Opens the door, sees his condition and is concerned.)*
24   **What happen to you?** *(PHANSO enters and stands in the*
25   *doorway. He is very agitated, very dusty and sweaty. He*
26   *wears ghetto-type street clothes complete with a "tam" on*
27   *his head and a rag dangling from his hip pocket. His*
28   *trousers are cuffless, they taper toward his ankles, and are*
29   *several inches short of his shoes. He is sockless. PUTUS cau-*
30   *tiously looks him over, then closes the door behind him.)*
31 PHANSO: **Long story.**
32 PUTUS: **Come inside, no?**
33 PHANSO: **I didn't see the woman's car, where she is?**
34 PUTUS: **Gone out as usual, so she not comin' back here for**
35   **now...though she know you comin' here at this time.**

1 PHANSO: *(Muttering)* No manners, no respec', that's what it is.
2 PUTUS: I suppose so. *(Pause)* Come inside, no?...So why you
3   stay like that? *(He doesn't respond but hesitates, reconsid-*
4   *ers, then walks into the room. He is uncomfortable.)* How
5   you get here? You walk?
6 PHANSO: Yeah. An' I have to get home before night.
7 PUTUS: Why?
8 PHANSO: This mornin' I had to beg Miss Gladys to look after
9   the children. She warn me not to stay till night, for she
10   have to go out.
11 PUTUS: I don't think she will allow them to go on the street
12   for she love them like her own.
13 PHANSO: You is their mother an' you can't keep them off the
14   street. How you expec' Gladys to keep them off the street?
15 PUTUS: *(Angrily)* How you expec' me to keep them off the
16   street from up here? That's now your responsibility.
17 PHANSO: *(Angrily)* I-man complain to you? *(A moment of*
18   *tension as they stare down each other. PUTUS doesn't want*
19   *a confrontation so she is torn between asking him to sit,*
20   *aware of his dusty and sweaty condition, and wanting to*
21   *avoid provoking an explosion.)*
22 PUTUS: You...you want to sit down? *(He does so.)* You hungry?
23 PHANSO: Slightly.
24 PUTUS: Let me fix you somethin' to eat. *(She exits to kitchen.)*
25   When you finish eatin', you goin' to have to wait outside,
26   for Miss Scarlett wouldn't like you to be in her house.
27 PHANSO: Yeah, I understan'. *(He appraises the room.)* So this is
28   how the other side of Jamaica live.
29 PUTUS: *(Offstage)* You don't see nothin' yet, milove. It's two
30   toilet this one apartment have. I suppose they make it for
31   somebody with diarrhea.
32 PHANSO: Rass bwoy, look at all this. An' me, you, Bright Eye
33   an' Sunshine have to live in one room. An' if anybody
34   want to piss at night, they better go into the yard to get
35   some relief.

1   PUTUS: *(Offstage)* **That's life, milove.**
2   PHANSO: **Somethin' is wrong somewhere an' I can't figure**
3   **it out.**
4   PUTUS: *(Offstage, in a measured voice)* **Well, politicians say**
5   **that the world divide up into the haves an' the have**
6   **nots...**
7   PHANSO: **Yeah. An' nobody have to ask which one I am.**
8   *(PUTUS enters with a plate heaped with food. She places it*
9   *before PHANSO and returns to kitchen.)*
10 PUTUS: **Let me get you somethin' to drink...** *(Pause)* **Phanso,**
11   **when you talkin' to Miss Scarlett, remember not to tell**
12   **her that you are my children's father, or she won't**
13   **employ you.**
14 PHANSO: **I am not an idiot, Putus.** *(PUTUS returns with a large*
15   *glass of pop and places this before PHANSO. She notices*
16   *dust on the table and blows noisily on it.)*
17 PUTUS: *(Annoyed)* **You dust from mornin' till night an' you**
18   **can never keep the place clean.** *(She attempts to dust the*
19   *table with her palm, then wipes it with her skirt. She inhales*
20   *and exhales loudly as she tries to blow the dust away.)*
21 PHANSO: *(Protecting his food, angrily)* **What you doin', woman?**
22 PUTUS: **Oh, sorry. I never mean the dust to come over there.**
23 PHANSO: *(Angrily)* **What you mean you never mean it? The**
24   **whole place cover with dust an' you never mean it? Now**
25   **the dust in my rass food.** *(Slamming the plate on the table)*
26   **How you expec' me to eat that?**
27 PUTUS: *(Angrily)* **I said I didn't mean it!**
28 PHANSO: **It's manners you don't have, Putus. No respec'. You**
29   **don't mean it. The whole world don't mean it. But who**
30   **end up with dust on them? Me. That's who.**
31 PUTUS: **Calm down, Phanso. Calm down.**
32 PHANSO: **What you mean, calm down? You blow dust on me,**
33   **you blow dust on my food an' I must calm down?**
34 PUTUS: **Phanso...what's wrong?...What went wrong today?**
35 PHANSO: **You do this kinda thing all the time, Putus.**

1   PUTUS: *(Shocked)* **Me?** *(Pause)* **No need to upset yourself. I'll**
2   **get you another plate of food, that's no problem.** *(She*
3   *takes plate and glass into the kitchen.)* **What time you leave**
4   **the house this mornin'?**
5   PHANSO: Five o'clock.
6   PUTUS: So Bright Eye an' Sunshine was sleepin' when you
7   leave?
8   PHANSO: Yes.
9   PUTUS: You fix their breakfast before you leave?
10   PHANSO: Yes, Putus.
11   PUTUS: Bright Eye still coughin' bad?
12   PHANSO: *(Controlled exasperation)* Yes, Putus. *(PUTUS returns*
13   *with another plate, this one piled even higher with food. She*
14   *gives the plate to PHANSO and places glass on the table.)*
15   PUTUS: You give him his medicine when it start?
16   PHANSO: *(Increasing exasperation)* Yes, Putus. *(PUTUS sits on*
17   *couch and ignores his tone of voice.)*
18   PUTUS: Sunshine knee heal up yet?
19   PHANSO: Yes, Putus.
20   PUTUS: You remember to put the hair grower on her hair?
21   PHANSO: Putus, if you was there in the house like you sup-
22   posed to, you wouldn't have to ask me all kinds of
23   questions.
24   PUTUS: Phanso, don't bother lose your temper. I am not livin'
25   in Miss Scarlett house as her maid because I want to. I am
26   livin' here because it's the only work I can get. You are
27   not workin'. It's nine an' a half months now you not
28   workin'...
29   PHANSO: You don't have to remind me...
30   PUTUS: Phanso, I am not complainin', it's just the facts. The
31   months I been livin' here, Phanso, is tough. It's tough on
32   me to be away from the children. Don't make it any
33   tougher...
34   PHANSO: I don't know how much longer I'm goin' put up
35   with this. Night come, you here, me there. When my

1   nature rise, what am I to do?

2 PUTUS: *(Angrily)* **What you expec' me to do? Stay home an'**

3   **starve with you?** *(While speaking, she throws her arms*

4   *forward in frustration and accidentally knocks over a cat-*

5   *shaped figurine which breaks in two on the table.)* **Shit! An'**

6   **the blasted woman goin' want me to pay for it.**

7 PHANSO: **Since you turn big-time-born-again-Christian, I**

8   **didn't know that you still swear.**

9 PUTUS: **That's how the devil provoke the newly delivered...**

10   **Thank you, Jesus.**

11 PHANSO: **Putus, you see this Jesus business? I warn you**

12   **already. It's been two long months of nothin' but Jesus. I**

13   **am gettin' tired of it.**

14 PUTUS: **Don't blaspheme, Phanso.**

15 PHANSO: **I am warnin' you.**

16 PUTUS: **You could warn all you want, Jesus is on** *my* **side.**

17

18

19

20

21

22

23

24

25

26

27

28

29

30

31

32

33

34

35

Downpayments

by Tracee Lyles

(Scene for two African-American women)

1   This play is a candid and insightful exploration into the lives
2 of Black women. Fancy is a slender actress in her mid-twenties
3 who is obsessed with pursuing a career in motion pictures; Nia is
4 also a slender and attractive woman in her mid-twenties, trying to
5 be a writer and bent on preserving everyone's integrity — but not
6 very adept at maintaining her own. The scene is after midnight
7 in Nia's room at Ruby's Roost, home to several Black women
8 sharing the comfort and camaraderie of this large, historic, ram-
9 bling house in L.A. Nia is typing at her desk when Fancy enters,
10 somewhat loaded from yet another amorous escapade with a
11 film executive whom she hopes will give her a part.
12
13 FANCY: *(Singing)* **There's no business like show business, like**
14   **no business I know La...da...da...da...da...dee...dee...**
15   **dee...da...when you are taking that extra bow. Hey, girl!**
16   **Que pasa? I might've known you'd be up...and writing**
17   **something. So what the hell else is new? I went dancing**
18   **up Beverly Hills way, got on down and got me a j.o.b. I am**
19   **hot, girl!** *(NIA looks up slowly.)* **I'm going to be in a televi-**
20   **sion movie.**
21 NIA: **Oh, you've had one of your evening auditions again.**
22 FANCY: **At least I got a job. What the hell you got?**
23 NIA: **Fancy, you must be more selective, you do have choices,**
24   **you know.**
25 FANCY: **Look, I've had enough preaching for one day. When**
26   **you gonna sell one of those mothers anyway? Always**
27   **holding up here thinking and writing, writing and think-**
28   **ing about being rell-lee-vont. Maybe if you ever sell**
29   **something, you can give me a rell-lee-vont role. Would**
30   **you do that for me, Nia, would you...hee, hee, hee. Me and**
31   **you friends, right? And friends supposed to tell each**
32   **other the truth, right? We used to be so close. What hap-**
33   **pened to us, Nia? Remember we used to talk all night long**
34   **about being rich, remember? Be honest, girl, wouldn't you**
35   **rather be rich than rell-lee-vont? No lies, just truth.**

1   NIA: No. And the truth is, Fancy, I could never trust you, or
2   depend on you. You want to remember, then remember
3   how irresponsible you were when I'd give you the money
4   to pay our rent and you took it and bought clothes, and
5   remember the money I loaned you that you never both-
6   ered to pay back. Money my parents sent me to live on. I
7   just got sick, sick and tired of being used. Now get out of
8   my room!
9   FANCY: No, you're the one who needs to get the hell out of this
10   room, and quick, too. Nia, we ought to double date the
11   way we used to, remember? Me and Sid, and he would get
12   a friend for you. But you'd call him Mr. Whitey, instead of
13   his real name. *(Pause)* Girl, you'd be in a hell of a fix, if
14   you ever fell in love with one, wouldn't you?
15   NIA: I pray for divine guidance not to ever, ever...again.
16   FANCY: What? Who, you? No shit, girl. Not you!
17   NIA: *(Thoughtfully)* I did once. At first it was all quite innocent
18   and casual, like most flirtations are. One thing led to
19   another and he set me up in a beautiful penthouse, with
20   two years of paid-up rent. We had some memorable
21   times. Suddenly, the warm and tender moments turned
22   into weekly warfare...bickering back and forth about
23   race, politics, religion, you name it. The beloved boudoir
24   became a brutal battlefield.
25   FANCY: What happened then?
26   NIA: I guess you could say I went searching. Not knowing
27   exactly what for. Then I met Batutta. He introduced me
28   to books about people and places I had never learned
29   about in the schools I went to. It was as if he knew at
30   once, without my saying it, that I had an unquenchable
31   thirst to find out about things. In my room, like a hungry
32   bear, I would devour the history of the so-called dark
33   continent and her golden glorious times, late into the
34   night. And the more I read, the more familiar I felt, yet I
35   felt new, too. I was eager to write my feelings down, and

1   oh, how I loved the words as they came to me. And while
2   I was casting off the old me, together we found the word,
3   "Nia." It means purpose, like the Nile River; and I took it
4   for my own.
5 FANCY: *(She has slipped into a good nod.)* N–i–a! It's such a
6   pretty name. My name don't have no deep meaning like
7   Nia. I always loved to dress up in pretty clothes. That's
8   how it started, because I loved to dress up. *(Her voice*
9   *trails off.)*
10 NIA: And it fits you to a tee, too. You are "Fancy"!
11 FANCY: You, too, girl. With your rell-lee-vont self. *(NIA covers*
12   *her with a blanket.)*
13 NIA: Good night, Fancy.
14
15
16
17
18
19
20
21
22
23
24
25
26
27
28
29
30
31
32
33
34
35

Live From the Edge of Oblivion

by Jerome D. Hairston

(Monolog for an African-American man)

1   This final monolog from the play sums up the conclusions
2   of the central Everyman-figure, Johnas, a young Black male
3   venting his frustrations about his chaotic neighborhood through
4   a school essay. The playwright surrounds Johnas with a variety
5   of urban types — Mutha Crackhead, Sir Hoodlum, Brother Wino,
6   and others — who purport to offer Johnas different value
7   systems, all of which he rejects. The playwright directs that at
8   the end of the monolog the national anthem be played very
9   loudly, suggesting that Johnas' conclusions about his future are
10 more than just the personal, depressing visions of an isolated
11 African-American: they reflect perhaps the outlooks of an entire
12 generation.
13
14 **"If My World Was Coming to an End," by Johnas H.**
15 **Gordon. Living in Sherton Square there are a number of**
16 **things I could do before my world ceased. There's always the**
17 **option of going down to the corner liquor store and buying**
18 **myself a cold forty ounce. Then I could go hang out with the**
19 **winos on the curb. I could just drink, drink, drink until I was**
20 **so messed up that I wouldn't even know my world was ending.**
21 **I could just clutch my bottle and laugh at a world I had no**
22 **place in anyway, scream my final words. After my last words**
23 **are spoken, one might ask, "Where will you go after your**
24 **screams fade away, and you stand alone, stranded in your own**
25 **echo?" I can always escape, catch the 11:59 glass rocket, and**
26 **fly to another world, one not known for return trips. But I**
27 **realize that price is too high. I still have the will to live and be**
28 **somebody. Who? I don't know. But, if someone is in the search**
29 **to survive, they search for any way possible. Maybe I need to**
30 **find that exit. Maybe then I could live through this apocalypse.**
31 **What better way to survive in a prison of oppression in pain,**
32 **than to become a part of it. As I look at my life now, I realize**
33 **there is no question about it. My world is coming to an end.**
34 **Maybe not today, or tomorrow, but my vision blurs when**
35 **trying to see the day after. I feel there's no chance of trying to**

1   hide the fact, or even trying to escape it. Hell, there's no use of
2   even trying to pray, because God's children don't seem to live
3   here anymore. So, what is left to do as the final hours draw
4   closer and closer? There's only one thing I can do. I'll lower
5   my head and cry now, for I know there will be no one here to
6   mourn after my people have faded away.
7
8
9
10
11
12
13
14
15
16
17
18
19
20
21
22
23
24
25
26
27
28
29
30
31
32
33
34
35

Cage Rhythm

by Kia Corthron

(Scene for two African-American women)

1   This play explores the experience of prison existence, as
2   seen through the eyes of two Black women inmates: T.J. and
3   Avery. T.J. is a lifer, desperately craving escape, and fascinated by
4   Avery's ability to "project" herself outside the prison walls by the
5   power of her mind. Avery says that she can occupy the body of
6   someone on the outside, using that body to go where she wants
7   and see what she wants. T.J. is skeptical. The focus of their
8   encounter here is how to deal with Avery's vanishing dream of
9   motherhood, as she nervously anticipates the visit of her eleven-
10   year-old daughter, Leesy, whom Avery hasn't seen in seven years.
11
12   **T.J.: I'm gonna leave. One day. Not take it anymore: gone.**
13   **AVERY: I ever tell ya my little girl liked her restaurant lunch?**
14   **T.J.: Just wanted to let you know.**
15   **AVERY: Once in awhile I treat her. Diner, we chat: my coffee,**
16   **her milk.** *(Pause)* **I be out five months, T.J. I had a lot left,**
17   **I'd be with ya. But I just got five months. Which ain't**
18   **plenty which means plenty to risk.**
19   **T.J.: I don't want you to! Like you to be with me, but you have**
20   **stuff to lose. I don't.**
21   **AVERY: Lose your parole.**
22   **T.J.: A maybe. A fat "if" and that's a conjunction I'm tired of**
23   **hearing.** *(Pause)* **Montana says you get out.** *(Pause)*
24   **Dreams?** *(AVERY shakes her head.)*
25   **AVERY: Takes concentration, but not much practice. Show ya**
26   **the book.** *(T.J., uneasy, shakes her head.)* **Yankees game,**
27   **box seats. Subway, 5:30 rush, sardines. Central Park. I**
28   **cool my feet in the pond.**
29   **T.J.: Wherever you want?**
30   **AVERY: Wherever there's a free body. You gotta find a body**
31   **whose spirit's out meanderin' just like you. Can't force**
32   **nobody's spirit out.** *(Pause)* **Believe me?** *(T.J. doesn't*
33   *answer.)* **Make your life easier. Seg.** *(Pause)*
34   **T.J.: I don't believe you, which is not to call you a liar. Wish I**
35   **did.** *(Pause)*

1   AVERY: Visitin' day, I help in the nursery. My first year, still
2   crack nervous, and this little boy keep talkin' 'bout his
3   daddy this his daddy that, I know he ain't got no daddy,
4   get on my nerves. So he grab the playhouse, I take it away.
5   He go to the train, I give it to the little girl. He grab the
6   jumprope, I snatch it call him Sissyboy he start to cry. All
7   the other kids is quiet, watchin'. His mama wanna kill
8   me, and she got a lotta influence 'round here. I ain't a bad
9   mother no more. One off day, I get nursery-expelled and
10   a reputation. I'm a good mother.
11   T.J.: I know.
12   AVERY: Do ya? *(T.J. nods. AVERY is pleased.)* Leesy comin'!
13   T.J.: When?!
14   AVERY: Tomorrow, four. Scared!
15   T.J.: Foster parents bring her?
16   AVERY: Sure, but she the one asked. Begged, for the longest
17   time, finally they grant it, see her mama. Meet her mama,
18   she won't know me, she's eleven, ain't seen me since
19   four. I'm shakin'.
20   T.J.: Normal, fine. Got all your stuff? Candy bars?
21   AVERY: *(Horror)* I ate 'em!
22   T.J.: Not a tragedy, she probably gets too much anyway. Your
23   sleigh?
24   AVERY: *(Rips apart her bed.)* I can't find it! I had it right here
25   under the sheets, that Randy got it in for me, she done it,
26   bet my life. *(T.J. moves towards the bed.)*
27   T.J.: Stop. *(AVERY backs away from the bed. T.J. calmly feels*
28   *under the bed; in a few moments pulls out the tape-dis-*
29   *penser sleigh. Santa has been torn. AVERY moans.)* You can
30   make another before tomorrow. Here. *(From under her*
31   *bed, T.J. pulls stationery and a ballpoint pen that clicks four*
32   *colors. Offers items to AVERY, but AVERY stares at pen.)*
33   Think Leesy like this pen? *(AVERY nods. Now she takes the*
34   *pad and pen and begins doodling.)* Better save the ink.
35   *(AVERY puts the pen in her pocket.)*

1   AVERY: If you get out, then me, can I stay at your place?
2   Awhile? I ain't got a roof now, and here's the Catch-22:
3   can't get my baby back no place to live, ain't eligible for
4   housing assistance if I ain't got child custody. *(T.J. nods.*
5   *Pause)*
6   T.J.: Why didn't you ever stay out there? In a free body?
7   AVERY: Be livin' somebody else's life. Somebody else's face in
8   the mirror.
9   T.J.: Somebody, anybody else's life beats this one.
10   AVERY: Still not mine. *(She looks at T.J.)* Noticed somethin'.
11   *(Pulls up her sleeve.)* My track marks are gone.
12
13
14
15
16
17
18
19
20
21
22
23
24
25
26
27
28
29
30
31
32
33
34
35

Mijo

by Michael Kearns

(Monolog for an African-American man)

1   This intense yet tender speech is spoken by Michael, a
2   young gay man, who is pleading with the mother of his lover, to
3   allow her son to die in peace from AIDS. He argues that death is
4   a release from pain, not an end to life. And that one of love's
5   strongest tests is the ability to "let go" of loved ones, when it
6   means "delivering" them from pain and suffering.
7
8   **Listen to your own sermon, Carmen: "Deliver us from**
9   **evil." That's all I'm asking. I'm asking you to deliver your flesh**
10   **and blood from evil. Deliver your baby from evil. Deliver your**
11   ***mijo* from evil. He cannot see; he cannot hear; he cannot laugh**
12   **– you must help him die. Don't you get it? That's why you're**
13   **here, to deliver him from evil pain; deliver him from evil suf-**
14   **fering; deliver him from evil torment; deliver him from this**
15   **hell on earth. If you love him, you will deliver him. If you love**
16   **him, you will release him. You don't know what loving**
17   **someone is until you deliver them from evil. I've loved a lot,**
18   **Carmen, and I've seen a lot of evil. When I was a little boy, we**
19   **lived on a street which butted up against a cemetery. To avoid**
20   **my half-dead family, I would escape there with a pack of bul-**
21   **lying school bruisers who delighted in deriding me. "Sissy,"**
22   **they'd venomously hiss. And believe me, the only thing worse**
23   **than being a white sissy is being a black sissy. We'd hide out**
24   **among the dead, proving our fearlessness – trying to pro-**
25   **nounce names on gravestones, sniffing gladiolas on the fresh**
26   **graves of the most recently departed and occasionally confis-**
27   **cating lavender or pink ribbons inscribed with the words "My**
28   **Brother" or "Dear Son" or "Loving Husband" made from**
29   **metallic gold stick-on letters. On one of our trips to the land of**
30   **the dead, we heard the whimpering sounds of a suffering**
31   **animal, buried in a pile of orange and amber leaves. Nearby**
32   **was the bloodied branch of a tree, remnants of a brutal St.**
33   **Louis storm the day before. The sturdy stick had obviously**
34   **struck the animal, wounding it without killing it. I couldn't**
35   **even see the crying animal – I think it was a squirrel – but I**

1 could feel its unremitting pain. What do we do? There was
2 only one moral choice: I must kill it, cease its endless lifeless-
3 ness, silence its cries. The other boys – champions of gym
4 class, heroes on the basketball court – were rendered unchar-
5 acteristically limp, deflated by the animal's helplessness. As
6 they scurried in all directions, I searched for a weapon,
7 finding a large rock, more like a boulder, which would deliver
8 the small beast from its misery. With all my might, I hurled
9 the rock in the direction of my pathetic victim, still hidden
10 under the autumn leaves, over and over again I threw it, until
11 there was no more sound. Never, in my short life, had I expe-
12 rienced such a stirring silence, such a staggering peace of
13 mind, such a stunning tranquility. At that very moment, the
14 sun appeared, illuminating the ground where I would bury
15 my prey. Using the very branch which had randomly targeted
16 the innocent animal, I dug a makeshift grave. Without ever
17 looking at the small creature, I scooted it into the grave,
18 admidst the sun-drenched golden leaves. For decoration, I
19 stole some blood-red gladiolas and a deep purple ribbon from
20 a nearby grave. I was no longer a powerless sissy. I was the star
21 now, a superstar of the cemetery. I became a man, in control,
22 who knew the difference between right and wrong, good and
23 bad, evil and spiritual. As quickly as it appeared, the sun evap-
24 orated and it began to sprinkle. In a frenzy of ecstasy, I ripped
25 off my clothes and danced in the pouring rain. The harder it
26 poured, the harder I danced. I must have danced until I
27 passed out from joyfulness. When I woke up, lying naked on
28 the grave of my loved one, it had stopped raining and the sky
29 was pitch black. I threw on my soaking wet clothes and stum-
30 bled over the freshly-muddied graves until I instinctively
31 found my way home. No one even knew I'd been gone and no
32 one cared about my elegiac epiphany. But I knew I would
33 never be the same. *(He removes several black candles from his
34 satchel.)* He loved candles. We'll place them around the bed.
35 We'll clean him up – bathe every inch of him like you did

1 when he was a little boy – in candlelight. *We* are going to
2 deliver him from evil. Put him to sleep. No more going to
3 honor him, like McDonald's Make a Wish Foundation. We are
4 going to give him what he wishes: deliverance.
5
6
7
8
9
10
11
12
13
14
15
16
17
18
19
20
21
22
23
24
25
26
27
28
29
30
31
32
33
34
35

Stop and Think

by Karmyn Lott

(Monolog for an African-American man)

1   On one level this play examines the influence of Malcolm
2   X's ideas on contemporary American society, now more than
3   thirty years following Malcolm's death. But on another level, by
4   introducing the character of "Malcolm X's Spirit," the play-
5   wright delivers a sharp critique of racism in the United States,
6   arguing that African-Americans only fool themselves by believ-
7   ing they're better off today than they were during the time of
8   slavery. The following monolog is spoken by the character James,
9   a young Black male about twenty years old, who recalls his own
10   upbringing in relatively comfortable circumstances — yet who
11   suffered from racist discrimination all the same.
12
13   **I was five years old. Big enough to play outside without**
14   **the supervision of my Irish nurse. I saw two young gentlemen,**
15   **Irishmen, they were playing outside. I said, "Hello," and**
16   **extended my hand because Father had taught me to do so.**
17   **Father said, "A gentleman, a true Bostonian gentleman,**
18   **always extends his hand first." Father has seen white gentle-**
19   **men do this and, of course, Father wanted me to be a**
20   **gentleman. So I said, "Hello," with my hand extended peace-**
21   **fully. "I'm Simeon Binney." The little five-year-old laddies**
22   **looked at me. They seemed somewhat surprised when I spoke**
23   **their language, Bostonian, of course. I heard one of them say,**
24   **"Will it come off?" Oh, silly boy, my hand will not come off.**
25   **But the little boy smiled and said, "The brown on your hand."**
26   **The other young laddie whispered, "Is it dirt?" "No," I said,**
27   **then I looked. But all I could see was a Bostonian hand, an**
28   **upperclass Bostonian hand. Suddenly the little boy with the**
29   **pink, cherry cheeks said, "Where do you come from?" "Over**
30   **there. I live in the finest house on the block. The one with the**
31   **best-set table, the corner house of the brownstone dwellings."**
32   **"No," said the cherry-cheeked boy, "I mean what country?"**
33   **"Boston," I said. "I'm a Bostonian. An upperclass Bostonian.**
34   **We all live on the same block. All Bostonians recognize other**
35   **Bostonians." The two Irish laddies looked at each other, then**

1   one of them whispered, "He's not a Bostonian." "But I am a
2   Bostonian," I said. Oh, they giggled and pointed. So I giggled
3   and pointed. We all laughed and laughed. Out of the midst of
4   their laughter I heard one of them say, "I think he's colored."
5   Me? A Bostonian, colored? Of course not. I'm a gentleman. A
6   Bostonian gentleman. An upperclass Bostonian gentleman. I
7   live in the house over there. The one with all the servants. I go
8   to private school. My father has money. That makes me a
9   Bostonian. The little Irish boy said, "No, you're not a
10   Bostonian." Then he showed me his hand. I felt so ashamed.
11   For Father had taught me always to be a gentleman, and I was
12   being a gentleman. My hand stood there just like a gentleman,
13   a Bostonian gentleman, but mine was tan.
14
15
16
17
18
19
20
21
22
23
24
25
26
27
28
29
30
31
32
33
34
35

An Asian Jockey in Our Midst

by Carter W. Lewis

(Scene for an African-American
man and woman)

1   This seriocomic drama explores the lives of minorities and
2   immigrants in the process of becoming assimilated into main-
3   stream American society. In this first scene from the play,
4   Nathan, a high school science teacher, and his wife attend the
5   opening of a Chinese restaurant at the race track they knew
6   when they were children. The present and the past begin to flow
7   together in fragments as the African-American couple is trans-
8   posed through time to become the Japanese family of an Asian
9   jockey that white crime is perpetrated against.
10
11 ALICE: Oh, just look at it all, Nathan. There's the clubhouse
12   turn. There's that mist rollin' in like a big sticky
13   marshmallow.
14 NATHAN: That must be one of those sportswriters up in that
15   plane.
16 ALICE: And there's those two little kids slippin' through the
17   mist like black cats on a white night.
18 NATHAN: How's a man supposed to concentrate with the
19   Blue Angels doing maneuvers over his table?
20 ALICE: Look, Nathan, all the cowboys are coming out to chase
21   that Indian. One, two, three, four, five, six, seven deputies
22   today, Nathan. Cowboys and Indians about to start.
23 NATHAN: This six horse is gonna run away with it.
24 ALICE: *(Grabs binoculars.)* Looky there. That woman looks
25   just like my momma.
26 NATHAN: We came out for a quiet lunch, don't go conjuring
27   up your momma.
28 ALICE: "You kids stay off the fence, or I'll let the horses stomp
29   your tiny little heads."
30 NATHAN: Your momma was always giving me that bad look.
31 ALICE: That's because you were always bad. You'd be
32   "yesmammin'" your way toward good and as soon as her
33   back was turned you were up on the fence yellin' at the
34   horses. "You the bad man, Sheriff's gonna get you!"
35 NATHAN: *(Laughs.)* "You the bad man."

1   ALICE: She'd be proud of you today, baby. She wouldn't give
2   you that bad look now.
3   NATHAN: That's 'cause she's dead.
4   ALICE: Hush, Nathan, she might be listenin'.
5   NATHAN: I'm sure she knows she's dead, Alice.
6   ALICE: You don't know what dead people know.
7   NATHAN: Well, if she don't know she's dead, she's spent the
8   last seventeen years wondering why we buried her.
9   ALICE: It's all so hocus-pocus. It's like the past is comin' to life
10   down there.
11   NATHAN: It's not hocus-pocus. You're rememberin'. Playing
12   movies on your eyelids. It's called mesmerism.
13   ALICE: I call it wishin'.
14   NATHAN: Mesmerism is good. It allows you to visit with your
15   momma without me having to arbitrate discussions on
16   whether tight shoes can cause flatulence.
17   ALICE: Wish we could see her again, do us some good.
18   NATHAN: Dr. Anton Mesmer believed you could, he believed
19   the world was permeated by a magnetic fluid that
20   records everything. The ebb and flow of that fluid is mes-
21   merism, which means soul measurement.
22   ALICE: I was just daydreamin', baby, no use in pullin' out no
23   dictionary.
24   NATHAN: The convergence of human energy in one spot is
25   called reunion theory.
26   ALICE: Nathan, to most of the world, energetic humans in one
27   spot is called a party. *(NATHAN looks at her over his eye-*
28   *glasses.)* Sorry, baby, I just want to enjoy coming here.
29   NATHAN: But that's what I'm talking about. Us coming back
30   here. Time's bitten off pieces of our souls and kept them
31   in nature's archives. We're nibbling at our souls just by
32   coming here.
33   ALICE: If we're nibblin' it's because we ain't seen a waiter,
34   and we ain't had lunch.
35   NATHAN: Don't say ain't, honey.

1   ALICE: Why not?

2   NATHAN: The wife of a man trying to move on, the wife of a

3   man trying to get elected to the school board, shouldn't

4   be putting her ain'ts where her isn'ts should be.

5   ALICE: Fine. We isn't seen a waiter and we isn't had lunch.

6   NATHAN: You know what I mean.

7   ALICE: "Ain't" was fine growin' up.

8   NATHAN: "Ain't" is reminiscent of the African-American

9   mammy cookin' hogs feet and black-eyed peas in a wood

10   shack.

11   ALICE: I don't care who cooks what where, I'd eat it. And we

12   ain't African-Americans anymore, we are people of color.

13   NATHAN: That terminology is not specific.

14   ALICE: I think "not specific" is the point. Nathan, we're colored

15   people again, but this time we got company.

16   NATHAN: It lumps us in with all those others.

17   ALICE: Who are you so afraid of lumpin' with?

18   NATHAN: I will not lump myself in with the Japanese. I will

19   not spend years fighting my way to the front of the bus,

20   only to find some model minority just bought it.

21   ALICE: Shush, Nathan. You shouldn't dislike the Japanese out

22   loud so much.

23   NATHAN: They're just white people who eat rice.

24   ALICE: It's those dreams you have.

25   NATHAN: My dreams are just dreams.

26   ALICE: Those dreams are why you have this thing about the

27   Japanese.

28   NATHAN: I do not have a "thing." It's a free country, I can

29   dislike whomever I please.

30   ALICE: Then why are we sittin' in this oriental restaurant?

31   NATHAN: It's Chinese. They're okay, they don't have as much

32   money.

33   ALICE: Well, I hope they got waiters.

34   NATHAN: "Have." I hope they "have" waiters. Alice, we're not

35   down on the fence anymore. We're here at the opening of

1   the China Rail Restaurant.

2   ALICE: Fine. Fine.

3   NATHAN: Are you upset about something?

4   ALICE: I'm not upset, I'm pregnant, it's different.

5   NATHAN: Then why you twisting your napkin like that?

6   ALICE: Like what?

7   NATHAN: Like you're doing.

8   ALICE: I'm wiping my hands.

9   NATHAN: That is an agitated motor response.

10   ALICE: Now you gonna show me how to wipe my hands?

11   NATHAN: Alice.

12   ALICE: I always twist my napkin this way. My momma used to

13   twist her napkin this way.

14   NATHAN: Alice.

15   ALICE: Come to think of it, my whole family used to twist

16   their napkins this way. After dinner, after the hogs feet

17   and watermelon rinds had been scraped onto the floor of

18   our woodshack, we'd all sit around twisting napkins

19   until dawn.

20   NATHAN: I'm sorry.

21   ALICE: You'd probably be president of the Board of Education

22   by now if it weren't for your low-class napkin-twistin' wife.

23   NATHAN: Maybe I should find a waiter.

24   ALICE: No, baby. Stay. Please? I want you to share this

25   with me.

26   NATHAN: Share what?

27   ALICE: Being here, Nathan. Remember with me. That's all I

28   want. Remember what we were like then.

29   NATHAN: *(Taking her hands)* I remember.

30

31

32

33

34

35

Tomorrow = x^2

by Myrtle Nord

(Scene for an African-American
woman and a Caucasian man)

1   The time is an evening in the summer of 1968, the locale is

2   on any city street, before the two houses of the Hickeys and the

3   Boltons. Russell Bolton is a young white Vietnam vet, and Diana

4   Hickey is the young daughter of the African-American family

5   next door. This is a lengthy and carefully choreographed poetic

6   love scene. Diana (woman) is on the front of the stage at far left,

7   as Russ (man) enters from right front. The woman draws back,

8   afraid. The man speaks. The two characters should move closer

9   to center stage, towards each other, one step at a time. The "aes-

10   thetic" quality of the scene should support both the political and

11   romantic themes that run through it.

12

13   **RUSS:** *(He takes a step towards her.)* **Hello. I'm Russell.**

14   **DIANA:** *(She returns the one step.)* **I am Diana.**

15   **RUSS: I wish I knew you.**

16   **DIANA: I wish I knew you, too. Russell?**

17   **RUSS: Diana?**

18   **DIANA: I am a non-person.**

19   **RUSS: Not a non-person. You have a job. Your father has a job.**

20   **Your brothers fight in the war. Your mother is a home-**

21   **maker. You live in America and this is who people are in**

22   **America.**

23   **DIANA: I am a minority.**

24   **RUSS: You are not minority. You live in a house. You have a**

25   **car. You are healthy and strong. You can read and write.**

26   **You are majority.**

27   **DIANA: I am black.**

28   **RUSS: You are colorless.**

29   **DIANA: I am colorless? And majority?**

30   **RUSS: Just as I am colorless, and majority. The highly suc-**

31   **cessful, the dismal failures – they are minorities, and**

32   **they are the ones with color. The unemployed, the dis-**

33   **loyal, the agitators, the prideless, the dishonest, the**

34   **criminal. They are the minorities. Even the intellectuals.**

35   **They are minorities. They have color. They are all in**

1   opposition. Opposition to something. But you and I...we
2   are the majority...but we have feet of clay.
3   DIANA: I do not understand. What does the majority do?
4   RUSS: Nothing. We are not in opposition to anything. We do
5   not seek power. We are not demanding anything we have
6   not earned. We do not ask for someone to do something
7   for us that we can do for ourselves. We are the peace of
8   the world, but we never say so. We are the happy, but no
9   one knows it. It is only self-interest that stirs upheaval
10   and creates a minority.
11   DIANA: I have no self-interest.
12   RUSS: I have so self-interest.
13   DIANA: Then why are there minorities?
14   RUSS: The minorities battle to become majorities. It is self-
15   satisfying...but for what? Only to find another minority
16   rising against them. No one wants to be majority because
17   majority is buried in holding the world together.
18   Majority is colorless, quiet, peaceful...maybe even
19   dull...but still we number the most. *(They should be about*
20   *four feet apart.)* Oh, Diana, if the majority ever stood up
21   together, we would rattle the bones in all the graves of all
22   the ages. But we do not stand up together.
23   DIANA: Then why are we lonely?
24   RUSS: I don't know.
25   DIANA: *(Crying out)* I am lonely!
26   RUSS: I am lonely, too! *(They reach out their hands to each*
27   *other and embrace, kissing.)*
28   DIANA: I don't want it to ever stop.
29   RUSS: We're not going to let it stop. We've found each other
30   and this much is ours! *(They turn and walk downstage*
31   *together.)*
32   DIANA: Can it really be?
33   RUSS: When life knocks at the door, no one can wait. Falling
34   in love is the touch of fate.
35   DIANA: You're being poetic. *(Laughing)* But it dazzles me!

1   **RUSS: I feel poetic. Oh, Diana, every moment I'm away from**
2   **you I ache...just to be with you again...to hold you in my**
3   **arms...to touch your cheek...your hair....** *(He embraces*
4   *her and they kiss.)*
5   **DIANA: Parting is such sweet sorrow....**
6   **RUSS: Oh, Diana, my own beautiful love. Do not run away so**
7   **soon. It's you I've been looking for...it's your voice I've**
8   **heard, and your face I've seen...in the battlefield at**
9   **night...I've dreamed of you...stay a moment longer....**
10   **DIANA:** *(Happily)* **You didn't even know me then.**
11   **RUSS: I didn't know where I'd find you...nor even where to**
12   **look for you...but I knew you. It's you, Diana...it's you I've**
13   **been searching for....**
14   **DIANA:** *(Soberly)* **Oh, Russell, the night songs are lovely and**
15   **you are very dear to me...but when the daylight**
16   **comes...and you and I stand side by side...so different....**
17   **RUSS: My precious one, do not let the fears of love line your**
18   **pretty face. I've seen the tenderness of life in the eyes of**
19   **women all across the land, and sea, but there are depths**
20   **in yours that I cannot let go.**
21   **DIANA: And I see the depths of you in yours...and I cannot let**
22   **go either....**
23   **RUSS: Then...then...you are mine...and I am yours....**
24   **DIANA: Yes...yes, my own....** *(Laughing, she kisses him lightly,*
25   *then breaks from him and races downstage.)* **Good night,**
26   **sweet prince...until it be tomorrow....**
27
28
29
30
31
32
33
34
35

Downpayments

by Tracee Lyles

(Monolog for an African-American woman)

1   This play is a candid and insightful exploration into the
2   lives of Black women. Fancy is an attractive actress in her mid-
3   twenties who is obsessed with pursuing a career in motion
4   pictures, and who has been "making the rounds" of the film
5   studios in the pathetic hope of landing a part. The earlier scene
6   between Fancy and her friend Nia revealed how close their rela-
7   tionship is. In this monolog, which occurs later in the same play,
8   Fancy pleads desperately with Nia to grant her a part in Nia's
9   new play. The scene is Ruby's Roost, home to several Black
10   women sharing the comfort and camaraderie of this large, ram-
11   bling, historic house in L.A. The time is the present.
12
13   **Audition...I don't mind auditions. Because I need this**
14   **one. Since we first met on the plane coming out here, you've**
15   **been reminding me that, "No matter what happens, keep your**
16   **dignity, Fancy." But you never understood I had dignity all the**
17   **time, and how I felt it beneath my dignity to do anything**
18   **except what I studied to do. I suppose it started the day my**
19   **mother made my first party dress. She spent most of her spare**
20   **moments at her machine sewing pretty things for me, so I'd**
21   **look like a baby doll. And when she dressed me up, I felt like**
22   **someone had sprinkled magic dust all over me. And then I'd**
23   **dance, sing, or do something on cue, and she'd rear on back**
24   **and clap her heart out. Momma never had no time to dress**
25   **herself up. Never had no time, only had time to work along-**
26   **side of Daddy. He said, "You spoiling that gal with those fancy**
27   **dresses, she'll never be fit for nothing but being fast." And I**
28   **was fast. So fast nobody could catch me. I was in one hell of a**
29   **hurry not to housekeep and chauffeur my life away like them.**
30   **I had a right to go after what I wanted. To be the best actress**
31   **in the world. All I heard was, "Don't do it, fool! You'll never**
32   **know where your next meal is coming from, you'll starve to**
33   **death." But there was no stopping me. I studied as hard as I**
34   **knew how in a dozen New York drama schools. Then the day**
35   **came I landed my first role onstage. And I was ready. Then on**

1 opening night, oh, how they clapped, just like my mother used
2 to. A big time critic called me "artiste," and he spelled it with
3 an "e," so you know I was legit for days. He wrote, and I quote,
4 "Miss Fancy Daniels invokes her beautiful voice and body
5 ever so intimately with her audience, they seem to touch like
6 lovers dining by candlelight," unquote. I wasn't no Fancy
7 freeze-frame then. And what have I done since? I'm no better
8 than those ten dollar "ho's" I been playing. But this role could
9 do it for me. It could take me back home. Back home...fur-
10 draped and chauffeur-driven. And I'd cruise all over every
11 damned body who said I'd never make it, so help me. So help
12 me? So help me, girl? Help me.
13
14
15
16
17
18
19
20
21
22
23
24
25
26
27
28
29
30
31
32
33
34
35

My Girlish Days

by Karen L. B. Evans

(Scene for two African-American women)

1   This tender scene deals with the blossoming of young love,
2   as Gertie shares with her friend Jenny the strange new emo-
3   tions she's been experiencing when she's with Sam. At first hurt
4   by Gertie's romantic secret, Jenny learns that it wasn't Gertie's
5   dislike of her, but her friend's own uncertainty and fear that
6   kept Gertie from telling Jenny. The period is early summer,
7   1936, the locale is the woods near Hallsboro, North Carolina,
8   and it is night.
9

10   **GERTIE: Come on, Jenny, stop dragging your feet. You'd think**
11   **you'd never had to walk over a patch of woods before!**
12   **JENNY: Where the hell are we going? And why do we have to**
13   **come out here in the middle of the night when God only**
14   **knows how many snakes and no telling what else is out**
15   **here?**
16   **GERTIE: It's only nine o'clock and whatever's out here is**
17   **more scared of you than the other way around. Take off**
18   **your dress.**
19   **JENNY:** *(Disgusted)* **Now if all we gonna do is smoke cigarettes,**
20   **why in hell couldn't we do it in our usual spot, instead of**
21   **trekking half way up this hill?**
22   **GERTIE:** *(Begins to take off dress.)* **Take off your dress.**
23   **JENNY: God knows I think you have lost your mind, niggah**
24   **woman. I got news for you, I could be home trying to**
25   **finish that stupid white dress for graduation I have been**
26   **struggling with eight going on nine days, I could be pol-**
27   **ishing my shoes, washing, pressing, or curling my hair,**
28   **and you, you have me way out yonder, past Mills Hollow**
29   **Road to what...to what?! To smoke a god damn cigarette!**
30   *(GERTIE has cleared a spot to sit and taken a small packet*
31   *from her bra.)*
32   **GERTIE: Jenny Anderson, have I ever led you on a wild goose**
33   **chase?**
34   **JENNY: Not up till this very moment. What is that?**
35   **GERTIE: Who got us the moonshine from Old Bob's still?**

1   JENNY: Uh, that won't no favor, I got sick as a dog behind that
2   stuff.
3   GERTIE: Who took you home and told your mama you got
4   sick at the county fair off somebody's chittlins they
5   hadn't cleaned right?
6   JENNY: You did. What is that?
7   GERTIE: Trust me, Jenny, 'cause I ain't never let you down.
8   JENNY: What is that?!
9   GERTIE: Take your dress off and rest a spell.
10   JENNY: Alright.
11   GERTIE: Now to be honest, I don't know exactly what it
12   is...but I do know that Grampa Barney goes out to the
13   woodshed late, rolls some of this and lights up. One
14   night, I couldn't sleep 'cause it was so hot, and I hear
15   Grampa Barney thumping on out to the shed. I tip out
16   after him. That woodshed's got so many gaps and holes
17   I'm surprised it keeps the wood dry. All I see is a red tip
18   of a cigarette glowing in the dark. And the funniest
19   stinky smell coming from the shack. And Grampa
20   Barney singing. On key. In a rich, deep voice.
21   JENNY: Your grampa?
22   GERTIE: Barnard Watkins.
23   JENNY: The man that united the gospel and youth choirs,
24   the ushers and missionaries in asking him to resign
25   from the church choir, and please not sing too loud in the
26   congregation?
27   GERTIE: Yep.
28   JENNY: What the hell is in that stuff?
29   GERTIE: I don't know, but let's find out.
30   JENNY: How'd you get it?
31   GERTIE: *(Amazed)* You can grow it! It was right between the
32   tomatoes and string beans. Looks like a bunch of weeds.
33   JENNY: Damn. *(They roll a cigarette and light up.)* Whew, wee,
34   this stuff stinks. *(Suspiciously)* You sure this stuff won't
35   make you blind or nothing?

1   GERTIE: He ain't blind, but he sure can sing!

2   JENNY: Hmmm. Where you tell your mama you were going
3   tonight?

4   GERTIE: Your place. What you tell yours?

5   JENNY: Your place.

6   GERTIE: Good thing those biddies haven't spoken to each
7   other in a year.

8   JENNY: Fighting like that over a cake. That's a shame.

9   GERTIE: God, I wish I had your mother.

10   JENNY: Well, she's no holy roller like your ma, but she's not
11   so hot.

12   GERTIE: You talk to your daddy about college again?

13   JENNY: *(Sullen)* Yeah, I don't know why I waste my breath. He
14   near 'bout killed me when he found out I'd gone behind
15   his back and applied to Tuskegee. He's saying the same
16   old thing. Don't no gal of his need to go to no college.
17   Waste of time, colored ain't never gonna get nowhere
18   no how.

19   GERTIE: You get somewhere if you're smart enough, and you
20   know that you and me are the two smartest things that's
21   lived in Hallsboro, North Carolina in a hundred years.

22   JENNY: Don't try and tell Miss Esther Norcum that! You know
23   she hates how we show up all the boys in algebra class. I
24   ain't never seen anybody crazier than that woman. Don't
25   think you should know anything but the pearls that drop
26   from her mouth. "Boys are better at math than girls, it's
27   natural." Crazy old thing.

28   GERTIE: Yeah, crazy like a fox. You see how she plays up to
29   Sam Williams? I can almost see her wrinkled old hands
30   start to sweat when she calls on him.

31   JENNY: Shame on you, Gertie. *(Slyly)* Maybe she's not the only
32   one who gets sweaty palms when Sam gets up in front of
33   the class. Roll me another one of those things.

34   GERTIE: What you talking about? Sam Williams can kiss my
35   butt. He don't want but one thing and I'll be damned if

1   I'll get knocked up and spend the rest of my life in these

2   woods.

3 JENNY: That's not the way it seemed when I noticed he was

4   just about the only one you was dancing with at the Dew

5   Drop last Saturday.

6 GERTIE: *(Defensively)* That's 'cause he practically wouldn't let

7   go of me.

8 JENNY: You managed to get away from boys before. If you

9   wanted to.

10 GERTIE: Why don't you work on your mama about college

11   'stead of your daddy?

12 JENNY: *(Takes a deep drag.)* How come you didn't tell me

13   about you and Sam.

14 GERTIE: There ain't nothing to tell, Miss Anderson. If there

15   was I woulda told you.

16 JENNY: Yeah, that's what I thought, too, so I waited...and

17   waited. I saw you two leave school together a couple of

18   times when I stayed late for Home Ec Club...then at the

19   Dew Drop. I ain't stupid.

20 GERTIE: Oh, Jenny, you know I've never kept anything from

21   you on purpose in my life.

22 JENNY: *(A little unsteady, JENNY walks away from her.)* Not till

23   now.

24 GERTIE: If I understood what was going on, I woulda told

25   you. You gonna listen?

26 JENNY: I'm listening, but I already know what I'm gonna hear.

27 GERTIE: What?

28 JENNY: *(With scorn)* That you're in love. After turning your

29   nose up at every little bama in this town who had the

30   hots for you that you suddenly realized that Sam

31   Williams is different, that Sam Williams is better than

32   the rest of them. *(She puts on her dress.)*

33 GERTIE: Why are you so mad?

34 JENNY: 'Cause it's all lies, Gert. I'll never get to college and

35   we'll end up here in Hallsboro with a bunch of babies

1 and growing tobacco and hoping the white man don't
2 lynch our men on hot Saturday nights.
3 GERTIE: It's not a lie! I'd never get your hopes up for some-
4 thing I didn't think could come true.
5 JENNY: We're fools. Young girls dreaming dreams, trying to
6 forget we're colored.
7 GERTIE: You're not being fair. *(JENNY doesn't answer.)* I
8 couldn't find the words to tell you. I thought you would
9 laugh at me so I didn't say nothing.
10 JENNY: I ain't never laughed at you in my life. That's my
11 problem. I take every word you say like it's gospel.
12 GERTIE: And I thought you'd be mad as hell.
13 JENNY: I could have laughed it off, if you had told me about it,
14 Gertie, why'd you lie?
15 GERTIE: Now, I didn't lie.
16 JENNY: You weren't straight with me for the first time and it
17 scared the shit out of me.
18 GERTIE: It scared me, too. *(Pause. She puts on dress.)* What
19 I'm trying to say is I don't know what's going on between
20 me and Sam. At first I could keep him at arm's length,
21 and I was cold and I was mean. Thought he was trying to
22 add another notch to his belt. But he kept coming back
23 for more, like a dog with a bone, he wouldn't let go, and
24 the worse I treated him the nicer he was. And then he
25 kissed me. And I couldn't hear Mama telling me to walk
26 with God, and I couldn't hear Miss Esther Norcum asking
27 me to do my homework over the way she taught it. When
28 he touches me, nothing matters. And I don't under-
29 stand...and I'm scared. *(A look of pain crosses her face.*
30 *JENNY comes and stands very close to her till they are*
31 *touching.)*
32
33
34
35

Off the Ice

by Barbara Field

(Monolog for an African-American woman)

1   This play is built on the story of the classic melodrama,

2   *Uncle Tom's Cabin*, where the runaway slave, Eliza, bravely

3   escapes her ruthless captors in the old South and flees to the

4   North. Here the playwright deepens the psychological portrait of

5   Eliza, eliminating the sentimentality and stereotyping that had

6   colored the original version. Eliza is now living in the home of

7   the March family in suburban Boston, 1866. The Civil War has

8   just finished and Eliza is a free person. In this monolog she tells

9   part of her story to the March sisters who listen raptly.

10

11   North, I run North. *(Sings.)*

12   *Run, nigger run, de patroller ketch you,*

13   *Run, nigger, run, it's almost day –*

14   I run – ran – north, steerin' by stars at night, sleepin' by

15   day. *(Sings.)*

16   *Over de hill and down de holler,*

17   *Patroller ketch nigger by de collar –*

18   I was born to the Shelbys.

19   No, I was owned by the Shelbys.

20   No, start at the beginning...and it's not the way you read

21   it in that damned book.

22   The Shelbys had a slave named Betty, she work in the

23   house, she warn't no field hand. One day the oldest Shelby boy

24   caught her in the kitchen garden. Which is how I was born.

25   Eliza. From birth, I had a solid place with Miz Shelby. I was

26   petted and spoiled – all my tasks was to shell peas and comb

27   the lapdog, and hem handkerchiefs for Miz Shelby. The old

28   lady had affection for me; she let me cut her toenails. When I

29   was twelve, that selfsame oldest Shelby boy who caught my

30   mama caught me. "Little girl, we gonna start a Nigger Farm,"

31   he said. We did, and that first baby (she born dead) I named

32   Beth. Soon he caught me again. Betsy. Dead. So the old lady

33   married me off to George from the next plantation. George, he

34   mean to me; we didn't make no babies, but that was no matter

35   'cause the oldest Shelby boy caught me in the kitchen garden,

1 which make Miz Shelby very cross! "Enough is enough!" So
2 she called Mister Haley, the slaver, to bring me to auction. Late
3 that night I stole some pone and bacon, and made me up a
4 little bundle of clothes. Miz Shelby knew, sure. She wanted me
5 to get away, only she be scared of all her menfolks. She won
6 me an hour head start by holding her tongue, and that's the
7 second-best gift she ever gave me.
8 *Dat nigger run, dat nigger flew,*
9 *Dat nigger tore her skirt in two,*
10 *Run, nigger, run, de patroller come...*
11 Run where? Up river to Ohio.
12 Past soldiers in gray and soldiers in blue.
13 Past bounty-hunters and patrollers too,
14 Slipped past, invisible, like I was a ghost.
15 Stopped long enough to bear a little boy, this past spring.
16 Scooped a little nest in the sand by a lake, and dropped
17 that boy in it like an egg. I wrapped him snug inside my
18 blouse, and ran some more.
19 *Run, nigger, run...*
20 North.
21 I headed north toward the place where the snow flies
22 and the ice grows thick on the water; north to the tundra and
23 past that to the pole, where there are no masters, no whip-
24 pings, no old ladies, no lapdogs, where the vista is white and
25 soft and hard. And safe, because it stays dark there all day
26 long.
27
28
29
30
31
32
33
34
35

Spirit Awakening

by Akuyoe

(Monolog for an African-American woman)

1   This is the concluding monolog of this one-woman play
2   tracing the development of self-identity in a young African woman
3   brought by her mother to the United States when she was a girl.
4   Highly poetic in style, it contains three sections marked here by
5   asterisks. It begins with a short, grim description of her childhood,
6   then erupts into an ecstatic realization of her African parents' her-
7   itage that has influenced her. Finally, it concludes in a jubilant
8   declaration of the "freedom" she has found in returning to her
9   roots as a spiritual being of African descent.
10
11 **Woman**
12 **black**
13 **so called weaker sex**
14 **conceived in rivalry**
15 **learned language of the opposition**
16 **gave up my own**
17 **chilling cold**
18 **mama working long hard hours**
19 **in the house we lived**
20 **a tension-filled house shared with friends**
21 **where the drunken stench and roar of the alcoholic**
22 **neighbor terrified his own and mine into a**
23 **graceless state of jaw-grinding silence**
24 **I was eight**
25 **caroline mensah was dead**
26 **it was night**
27 **the grown ups had gone to mourn**
28 **I was alone in my room**
29 **I was afraid**
30 **mr. cunningham was only days dead**
31 **kofi was a close family friend**
32 **he lived in the basement**
33 **he was twenty-seven**
34 **he was a man**
35 **he was to comfort and protect me**

1   I was a child
2   I was eight
3   infant strength
4   trust abused
5   his comfort an act of perversion
6   I closed my eyes
7   feigned sleep
8   held my breath
9   tears caressed my face
10   screams strangled in my throat
11   his fingers
12   cold
13   probing
14   their carnal deed to do
15   my stubborn thighs a closed gateway
16   his attempted rape
17   my shame
18   my rage and secret pain
19   inability to stand up for myself
20   unspoken
21   finally spoken
22   nineteen years
23   breathing
24   talking
25   talking back
26   understanding myself
27   ***
28   Free
29   the beautiful ones are yet born
30   they disguise themselves and then the angels can't recognize
31   them anymore
32   mama
33   what lessons and challenges have you buried deep in your
34   womb?
35   endurance isn't always strength

1   yielding too has its place and beauty
2   let's share you and I
3   a help one to another
4   ending this reign of victimhood
5   I see now that I judged you cruelly
6   the pain I feel
7   not being enough
8   you too have been feeling for years
9   your spirit hungering for empowerment
10 how were you to know this would lead
11 you to a barren land where friendships were a luxury
12 and your ebon skin a branding worse than the scarlet letter
13 you had to play your highlife and wear your bright colors
14 to keep a sense of who you were
15 papa
16 when I gave my blessed name did I also give up the part
17 of you in me?
18 all your silence
19 perhaps you've been trying to talk to me
20 perhaps in your silence you were trying to tell me secrets
21 a scornful mother that neglected you
22 a starched father that stifled you
23 sights and sounds of colonial rule which stilled your tongue
24 and made your heart fearful
25 papa I'm listening
26 hum like the wind, pitter patter like the rain
27 roar like a mama lion
28 island in the sun is this the face of the motherland you wanted to
29 see?
30 me and my "good" hair are moving on
31 giles you've been playing a part I allowed you to play
32 I want to breathe like a feather
33 dream rainbows
34 greet the sun
35   ***

1   Boldness fill me with your cool purple hues and long legged
2   strides
3   take my spirit upon your wings and let's fly over carmine sunsets
4   as we glide through symphonic waves
5   maybe we'll land in china for a glimpse of that last emperor
6   or on a tahitian island where i'll borne brando's tenth child
7   it's in my blood
8   my father had sixteen
9   we'll have no worries boldness and I
10   we're giving our lives over to Highest Creative Force
11   and in that surrender depositing all worry and fear for an
12   awesome, brow-raising, eye-popping, mouth-dropping
13   moment-to-moment livingness
14   the saboteur's spell broken
15   I'll no longer delay my life with my chronic latenesses
16   and upon arrival compare and tell myself that I'm not
17   "good enough"
18   reclaiming a child-like appetite for the spontaneous and
19   simple
20   I am
21   Papa
22   we are
23   i'd forgotten but now I see
24   I am
25   mama
26   we are
27   born in the image of mother africa
28   desecrated this beauty
29   with a mask of illusion
30   glory be
31   Ataa–Na Nyonmo
32   mi da boshi
33   [Father Mother God
34   I thank you]
35   drums talk that talk

1   **let the hallelujah chorus sound**
2   **for now unto forever more**
3   **I am**
4
5
6
7
8
9
10
11
12
13
14
15
16
17
18
19
20
21
22
23
24
25
26
27
28
29
30
31
32
33
34
35

Five Scenes From Life

by Alan Brody

(Scene for an African-American man
and a Caucasian woman)

1   This is a prison drama, a love story between a young, white
2   university teacher who volunteers to teach in a federal prison,
3   and a young black male who, unknown to her, is serving a very
4   long sentence for murder. The scene is a small, unadorned class-
5   room just following the end of Nina Shenton's Government
6   class. One of her students, Bobby Jones, has remained after the
7   other convicts have left, supposedly to explain why his assign-
8   ment was not turned in. Mike, the guard, is waiting in the
9   hallway outside.
10
11   NINA: You're going to be late for lock-up.
12   BOBBY: I got permission.
13   NINA: Trusty?
14   BOBBY: Sort of. *(Pause)* **My paper's not in there. Somebody**
15   **ripped off my books. I was going to do a thing on the Bill**
16   **of Rights, you know? But somebody ripped it off. The**
17   **book.**
18   NINA: Not the bill.
19   BOBBY: You think I could have yours?
20   NINA: What about the library?
21   BOBBY: It's hard to get time.
22   NINA: You can find it.
23   BOBBY: I just wanted you to know why it's late. Is that OK?
24   *(NINA gestures as if to say there's nothing she can do about*
25   *it.)* You're a good teacher.
26   NINA: Thanks.
27   BOBBY: You don't take no shit. Like when Abingdon was
28   doing his number on civil rights and you told him...what
29   did you say?
30   NINA: I just stopped him.
31   BOBBY: You said this course wasn't Black Rage 101 and if he
32   had a point to make he should make it. That was tough.
33   NINA: I wouldn't have stopped him if I believed him.
34   BOBBY: That's what I mean. He does that number in every
35   class. You're the first one to ever stop him. You know

1   what he's in for?

2   NINA: I don't want to know what anyone's in for.

3   BOBBY: You don't bullshit us, either. Some of the other dudes

4   come in here, you know. We can tell they're not giving us

5   the same shit they're giving the kids at the college.

6   Scaling down, y'understand me? Like intellectual

7   welfare. Mr. Garifole. You know him? *(NINA nods. BOBBY*

8   *waits for more.)*

9   NINA: He's a little tense.

10   BOBBY: He would have given me his book.

11   NINA: Testing me?

12   BOBBY: Just pointing out the distinction. *(Pause)* Is this what

13   happens after your class? You wait in here till they take

14   you out?

15   NINA: Or in the hall.

16   BOBBY: That's rough, huh? Everybody checking you out.

17   NINA: Get your paper in next week. OK?

18   BOBBY: See, that's what I mean. No shit lady. Could I ask you

19   a personal question?

20   NINA: No.

21   BOBBY: How come you do this? I mean, it's easy to figure out

22   a lot of the other dudes. Who's doing it for the extra

23   bread, or out of, you know, guilt or politics. Bunch of

24   guys locked up here for murder and rape and doing

25   drugs and shit like that, and you come in once a week to

26   give us a college education.

27   NINA: I wanted to know what it was like. Whether there was

28   really any difference.

29   BOBBY: Difference?

30   NINA: You spend your life teaching the system to kids who've

31   been protected by it, it's a good idea to check out how it

32   works for the ones who weren't.

33   BOBBY: Want to find out what it's like to be black, too, huh?

34   NINA: What it's like to be white.

35   BOBBY: That's cool. That's exceptionally cool.

1   NINA: Why?

2   BOBBY: No do-good crap.

3   NINA: That's not my style.

4   BOBBY: Right on. Is there?

5   NINA: What?

6   BOBBY: A difference.

7   NINA: Not a lot. Same late papers. Different excuses. You can't

8   go to your grandmother's funeral all the time.

9   BOBBY: You don't believe me about the books.

10   NINA: It doesn't matter. The paper's late.

11   BOBBY: Hey. That's very existential. Am I making you

12   nervous?

13   NINA: Why?

14   BOBBY: Staying in here alone with you.

15   NINA: Mike is out there.

16   BOBBY: You are one cool lady.

17   NINA: Get your paper in next week. OK?

18   BOBBY: Any pointers?

19   NINA: Keep it simple.

20   BOBBY: Yeah.

21   NINA: And honest.

22   BOBBY: Mr. Chatsworth. You know him? That's all he wanted

23   in freshman English. Simple and honest. He had a lot of

24   rescue fantasies.

25   NINA: How did you do?

26   BOBBY: OK.

27   NINA: What's OK?

28   BOBBY: OK is OK.

29   NINA: I think you better get back now.

30   BOBBY: Yeah. One other thing. Next weekend. We got this

31   thing. Family Day. Anybody tell you about that?

32   NINA: No.

33   BOBBY: The busses come up from the city. Wives and kids

34   and mothers and aunts and ladies, if they're still inter-

35   ested. And they get here with all these shopping bags,

1 see, and they're filled with barbecued chickens and cole
2 slaw and brownies. And presents like electric razors and
3 8 x 10 portraits of the kids in full color and bunches of
4 cloth flowers that somebody's made who couldn't make
5 it up to, you know, brighten up the block. And when they
6 get here they have to lay it all out before they come in so
7 they can be sure nobody stuffed a barbecued chicken
8 with any shit or made the flowers out of cigarette paper.
9 So it takes a couple of hours for them all to get in 'cause
10 everybody has to wait in line until they take out the cole
11 slaw and the brownies and the electric razors and the
12 pictures and then put it all back in — except for the metal
13 detectors which also takes a long time because the nails
14 in somebody's shoes always sets the damned thing off
15 and then they have to do a body search. Then everybody
16 goes into the gym where they set up a bandstand and a
17 bunch of the cats play and some of the cats' ladies sing,
18 except they're already tired from the bus ride and the
19 taking out and the putting back and taking out again,
20 and now they don't have as much time as they thought
21 they would so everybody's trying to be happy fast and
22 they get right down to the bump...
23 NINA: What?
24 BOBBY: ...Bump. It's a dance. A little old-fashioned, but it
25 does what we need it to, so we hang onto it here. Anyway,
26 there's all these little kids dressed up to see their daddies
27 in jackets and ties and short pants or little starched
28 dresses and ribbons and their hair all pulled tight in
29 braids and cornrows and they end up running all over
30 the gym because Mommy and Daddy or whoever are
31 busy doing the bump. Except some of the other little kids
32 do it, too, like imitating. Then somebody makes a speech
33 for the local NAACP and somebody else for the Muslims
34 and they welcome all the visitors and tell them they hope
35 they had a good time and to please contribute or join the

1   NAACP or the Muslims. And by that time the little kids

2   are all stained with chicken drippings and cole slaw and

3   chocolate cake and they're tired from the bus ride and

4   the waiting and doing the bump and they're bored with

5   the speeches, so they're crying and getting slapped. Then

6   they send them all back to the busses. So everybody says

7   good-bye and hugs each other fast 'cause the busses are

8   waiting and the bells are going to ring for lock-up and

9   they got to do a body search on all of us to make sure

10   nothing got by when they checked outside and everybody

11   says how they can't wait for the next month. And that's

12   Family Day.

13   NINA: Sounds like the faculty picnic.

14   BOBBY: Except for the body search.

15   NINA: And the bump.

16   BOBBY: So you want to come?

17   NINA: What?

18   BOBBY: Next weekend.

19   NINA: I don't think I'd...

20   BOBBY: Hey, I'm asking if you'd like to be my family.

21   NINA: That's very sweet.

22   BOBBY: Don't bullshit me.

23   NINA: Hey.

24   BOBBY: "Very sweet" is bullshit.

25   NINA: All right. No.

26   BOBBY: Why not?

27   NINA: You just asked me for what I think was a date, and I

28   said no. I don't have to explain.

29   BOBBY: I asked you to be my family.

30   NINA: Wife, mother, aunt, or lady?

31   BOBBY: *(Suddenly vulnerable)* Just...a friend.

32   NINA: I'm sorry. *(She means it.)*

33   BOBBY: It's OK.

34   NINA: You don't have any family?

35   BOBBY: A lot of guys like that. Used to be they wouldn't even

1   let us into the gym if we didn't have visitors. Now they do.

2   So we hang around some friend's family — not too long,

3   though, 'cause they want to get some time alone with

4   each other, so all the guys with no visitors end up horsing

5   around on one side of the gym like those girls who used

6   to dance with each other at the high school hops. You

7   know what I mean?

8 NINA: Very well.

9 BOBBY: So I just thought I'd ask.

10 NINA: It wouldn't be too smart a move.

11 BOBBY: Why not? *(Quickly)* OK if I ask this time?

12 NINA: *(Smiles.)* It would be unprofessional.

13 BOBBY: You could figure it's part of my rehabilitation.

14 NINA: I'm not here to rehabilitate you. All I do is teach

15   Government 103.

16 BOBBY: That's not all you do.

17 NINA: There would be other students there. What do you

18   think they'd make of it if I showed up as your...friend?

19   And what would that do the next time I walked in here?

20 BOBBY: You got somebody on the outside?

21 NINA: *(Quickly)* No.

22 BOBBY: Hey, I don't believe you.

23 NINA: Hey, I think this conversation's over.

24 BOBBY: You're not stringy.

25 NINA: What?

26 BOBBY: You know how some women have these skinny necks

27   with all the bones showing like they're always one step

28   ahead of a scream? That's stringy. It comes from being

29   alone. You're not like that. So I don't believe you. I tell

30   you what. Bring him along. Then you don't have to worry

31   about the class. He can hang around with the other cons

32   while we do the bump.

33 NINA: I'm going to wait in the hall.

34 BOBBY: I'll wait with you.

35 NINA: Don't come on to me, Bobby.

1   BOBBY: See? That's what I said. No shit, lady.
2   NINA: I don't think I sent out any signals, but if I did, you
3   misread them. And I tell you what. Just to make sure
4   we're clear, watch your language around me.
5   BOBBY: I didn't mean to make you mad.
6   NINA: I also know about put-ons.
7   BOBBY: *(Quickly)* I meant it. I wanted to invite you...
8   NINA: Not then. Now. You're too arrogant to be contrite.
9   BOBBY: I blew it.
10 NINA: I'm calling Mike.
11 BOBBY: So did you. *(She hesitates. He moves in quickly.)* You
12   lost your cool. You knew what to expect when you started
13   teaching up here. You probably had training sessions on
14   what to wear and how to handle the love poems and the
15   sexy letters and the guys checkin' to see whether you got
16   a bra on and the looks in our eyes that tell you what's
17   going on behind them, and they taught you how not to
18   take it personal, because after all, the cons don't get to
19   see a lot of women so you have to understand it could be
20   anybody. But it's nothing a smart, mature lady with a
21   Ph.D. can't handle. Right? But you did take it personal, so
22   you blew it, too.
23 NINA: You're right. I'm sorry.
24 BOBBY: Wrong. It was personal.
25 NINA: Oh, for Christ's sake...
26 BOBBY: No. Listen. I mean I *like* you. That's all I'm trying to
27   say. I'm not talking about dirty pictures. I'm not talking
28   about goons like Mendes who got their hands in their
29   pockets all the time. I'm talking *like.*
30 NINA: Look, Bobby...
31 BOBBY: Just let me tell you. We've had lady teachers before.
32   And I've sat there with all the other goons watching
33   movies in my head while she talked about the English
34   Romantics or supply and demand and thought she was
35   doing just fine in the field. I came in here all ready to use

1   you like that, too. But you arrive dressed, you know, just
2   right with that blouse buttoned so your neck was open
3   and the collar fell so that was all. Not scared, not pushy.
4   Just right. And you got down to business. We could tell
5   you knew what we were thinking, and you just let us.
6   And, yeah, I was thinking it, too, but it kept turning into
7   something else. Every time you smiled when some other
8   lady teacher would have laughed too hard, or when you
9   listened to one of us and came back – bam – dead on the
10   target so it showed you were really listening, I could feel
11   it turn into something else. I thought, hey, I like this lady.
12   I'd like to *talk* with her. So I just wanted you to know. You
13   make me feel warm without burning, y'understand me?
14   That's all I meant. And I wanted to tell you. *(Long pause)*
15 NINA: How does it work? Family Day?
16 BOBBY: You sign this request. See? Inmate: Bobby Jones,
17   number 69-D-0591. Then you put down your name here.
18   Visitor: Dr. Nina Shenton. I give it to the Family Day com-
19   mittee. You're already cleared for up here, so that's all.
20   You just arrive about 10:00 a.m. with your regular pass.
21 NINA: Give it to me. *(She sits down with her roll book.)*
22 BOBBY: What are you doing?
23 NINA: Adding some names. I'll come as a guest of the class.
24   Can you let them know that?
25 BOBBY: One smart lady.
26 NINA: Read them out to me.
27 BOBBY: Abingdon, Edward, number 76-D-4723; Mendes,
28   Rafael, number 43-B-0211; Napoli, Tony, number 34-C-
29   9652; Washington, James, number 62-C-0479....
30
31
32
33
34
35

Jelly Belly

by Charles Smith

(Scene for an African-American man and woman)

1   This award-winning play deals with the problems that
2   hard-working, middle-class African-Americans encounter today
3   as they try to build decent lives for themselves and their chil-
4   dren in modern American society. Mike, a construction worker,
5   and Barbara, a homemaker, are a young married couple living in
6   their house in the inner city. It is early evening and Barbara is
7   sitting on their front porch as the scene opens.
8
9   **BARBARA:** *(Calling to a boy offstage)* **Hey, boy! You! Yeah, I'm**
10   **talking to you. What you doing messing with that car? I'll**
11   **tell you one thing, you better leave it alone. What? I know**
12   **your momma. I'll beat your ass. I'll beat your ass, take**
13   **you home, and then your momma'll beat your ass. That's**
14   **right, go on about your business. Go ahead.** *(Under her*
15   *breath)* **Hard-headed little son of a bitch, you.** *(MIKE*
16   *enters.)*
17   **MIKE: Kenny here yet?**
18   **BARBARA: Nope.**
19   **MIKE: I wonder what happened to him.**
20   **BARBARA: He's probably mad at you.**
21   **MIKE: Want another beer? Last two.**
22   **BARBARA: Thanks. He asleep?**
23   **MIKE: Out like a light.**
24   **BARBARA: He ought to sleep good tonight. Had a full day.**
25   **MIKE: He was telling me about it. Said he wants to go back**
26   **tomorrow.**
27   **BARBARA: That's good.**
28   **MIKE: Rough, huh?**
29   **BARBARA: For a while there, I didn't think we was going to**
30   **make it. God, I didn't know a little boy could be so full of**
31   **questions. "Is the school really big, Mommie? Mommie,**
32   **will we have cookies and milk at school? Can I take my**
33   **dog to school, Mommie? Mommie, do they have bath-**
34   **rooms there?" We got there, he stopped, looked around,**
35   **folded his arms, nodded his head, looked up at me and**

1   said, "Thank you, Mother. I think I'm ready to go now." I
2   tried to explain to him, no, Mike, this is school, remem-
3   ber? You have to stay. But he wasn't having none of that.
4   MIKE: Did he cry?
5   BARBARA: At first.
6   MIKE: What you do?
7   BARBARA: I told him that if he wanted to be like his daddy, he
8   couldn't cry.
9   MIKE: And it worked?
10   BARBARA: Works every time.
11   MIKE: I wish you wouldn't tell him that. *(To a boy offstage)*
12   Hey, boy! What you doing messing with that car?
13   BARBARA: That's that little Paterson boy.
14   MIKE: *(To boy)* You better get away from that car.
15   BARBARA: I done told him once.
16   MIKE: *(To Barbara)* Somebody ought to talk to that boy's
17   momma.
18   BARBARA: She don't care what that boy does.
19   MIKE: *(To boy)* Go on home, boy! Watch TV or something. Go
20   ahead! *(MIKE and BARBARA watch the boy leave.)* Damn
21   shame.
22   BARBARA: Somebody don't set that boy straight, he's going to
23   end up in prison, you mark my words.
24   MIKE: I wish Kenny would get here. I'm ready to go to bed.
25   BARBARA: Will you stop worrying about Kenny? Kenny's
26   going to have to learn how to take care of himself.
27   MIKE: Maybe I ought to call to see if he's at home.
28   BARBARA: Mike? Sit down and cool out, OK? *(MIKE sits.)* I
29   called my father.
30   MIKE: For what?
31   BARBARA: Just to talk.
32   MIKE: Shit.
33   BARBARA: Mike...
34   MIKE: I wish you wouldn't have done that.
35   BARBARA: He's my father.

1   MIKE: Yeah.
2   BARBARA: I'm allowed to talk to my father, ain't I?
3   MIKE: It depends.
4   BARBARA: On what?
5   MIKE: On what you two talked about.
6   BARBARA: We didn't talk about nothing. We just talked.
7   MIKE: Yeah, OK, just talked.
8   BARBARA: Mike, if you don't want to go back, you don't
9   have to.
10 MIKE: Right.
11 BARBARA: You could find another job.
12 MIKE: Where?
13 BARBARA: Anywhere. There are places out there that would
14   hire you in a heartbeat.
15 MIKE: Everybody's cutting back.
16 BARBARA: But you've got experience.
17 MIKE: Everybody's got experience.
18 BARBARA: You don't have to take this shit from them, Mike.
19   With all of the construction going on in this town, you
20   could find a job paying twice what you're making now.
21 MIKE: I already looked. There was nothing in the paper. I
22   went down to the unemployment office, but there was a
23   line. I can't see myself standing in line all day.
24 BARBARA: Then I'll get a job.
25 MIKE: You?
26 BARBARA: Damn right, me.
27 MIKE: Doing what? Working with your father?
28 BARBARA: I don't have to. I can do other things.
29 MIKE: Yeah. Type.
30 BARBARA: They call it administrative management, baby.
31   Director of Interoffice Communications.
32 MIKE: Typing.
33 BARBARA: Don't knock it, baby. Typists make lots of money.
34 MIKE: Yeah, like your last job.
35 BARBARA: That's not quite what I had in mind.

1 MIKE: Call them. I'm sure they'll be glad to have you back.
2 BARBARA: That bitch was crazy, Mike.
3 MIKE: Tell me about it.
4 BARBARA: Come rubbing up on me telling me how I can
5   increase my cash flow.
6 MIKE: You should've told her something.
7 BARBARA: I did. Told her she didn't have enough cash to be
8   getting into my flow.
9 MIKE: So call her. Yeah, that'll be nice. You call up the dyke
10   and I'll quit my job and stay home with the kids.
11 BARBARA: I'm serious, Mike. You don't have to go back. If
12   worse came to worse, I could always go to work for my
13   father.
14 MIKE: See? That's what I thought.
15 BARBARA: Come on, Mike...
16 MIKE: That's exactly what he wants. For you to go to work for
17   him. His little girl. No. Absolutely not.
18 BARBARA: So I can go someplace else.
19 MIKE: Why you so set on getting a job? You don't have to go to
20   work. Not unless you really want to. I mean, if that's what
21   you want to do, say so. It's fine, by all means, go right
22   ahead. But you told me you wanted to stay home with
23   Mikey. And I mean, hell, we're doing all right. We got a
24   little money in the bank, we don't owe nobody nothing,
25   no where, no how. We are three steps ahead of everybody
26   else who are two blocks behind. I mean, we're not doing
27   that bad, Barbara.
28 BARBARA: I just want to make sure you don't have to do any-
29   thing against your will.
30 MIKE: I am doing exactly what it is I want to do. I am going
31   back tomorrow and act like nothing ever happened. I'm
32   going to be all smiles, handshakes, and grins, 'cause
33   right now, that's exactly where I need to be. But the day
34   is going to come when I won't need them anymore. The
35   day is going to come when I'm going to be my own boss,

1   have my own company, and that's the day I'm going to
2   walk into that office and tell them to kiss my ass. But
3   until that happens, I cannot quit, I will not quit, it's going
4   to take a lot more than this to knock me down.

5   BARBARA: Does this mean I have to stay home now?

6   MIKE: Not if you don't want. You can go back to work for the
7   dyke if you want.

8   BARBARA: Well, you know...she and I did have a certain
9   rapport.

10   MIKE: So call her.

11   BARBARA: You don't mind?

12   MIKE: 'Course not.

13   BARBARA: You sure?

14   MIKE: Positive. You just have to find you someplace else to
15   live, 'cause you sure as hell ain't staying here.

16   BARBARA: Boy! *(BARBARA slaps MIKE about the head. MIKE*
17   *tries to duck.)*

18
19
20
21
22
23
24
25
26
27
28
29
30
31
32
33
34
35

SCENES AND MONOLOGS
of the Asian-American Experience

Struggling Truths

by Peter Mellencamp

(Scene for one Asian and one Caucasian man)

1   This play portrays the emerging situation of Tibet in the
2   modern world by contrasting the values of western European
3   and Chinese societies with those of Tibet. In this humorous
4   scene, a surprisingly westernized Dalai Lama encounters a
5   Mountaineer from Austria who is seeking political asylum in the
6   Himalayas in 1940. The Dalai Lama has heard of the man's
7   arrival and has granted him a personal audience. The
8   Mountaineer finally discovers the Dalai Lama in the Potala
9   Palace courtyard where His Holiness is trying to repair his
10   orange '31 Dodge.
11
12   **MOUNTAINEER:** *(Bowing)* **Your Holiness, please pardon me, I**
13   *— (The DALAI LAMA rushes over to him.)*
14   **DALAI LAMA:** *(Clapping his hands)* **You are the man who**
15   **climbs mountains, from Europe! I've been waiting so**
16   **long to meet you! How do you do, I am the Dalai Lama!**
17   **MOUNTAINEER: Yes, I —**
18   **DALAI LAMA: — I have so many questions! And you can teach**
19   **me, you must know so many things the lamas don't!** *New*
20   **things!**
21   **MOUNTAINEER:** *(Glancing behind him offstage)* **I don't think**
22   **the lamas** *want* **me to teach you any new things, your**
23   **Holiness —**
24   **DALAI LAMA:** *(Pulling him toward the car)* **I know, I know,**
25   **they don't like any idea unless it's a hundred years old.**
26   **They had a fit when I told them to bring this machine out**
27   **of storage** *— (Kicking the tires fondly) —* **it's got wheels, you**
28   **know.** *(He stands next to the car, putting his hand on the*
29   *fender proudly.)* **It's a "Nineteen-Thirty-One-Dodge." It**
30   **was given as a present to my former body. It's the only**
31   **one in all of Tibet.** *(He drags the MOUNTAINEER around*
32   *to the engine.)* **...And nobody in all of Tibet knows how it**
33   **works! I've taken the whole thing apart and put it back**
34   **together again, but I still don't understand it, not all of it.**
35   **You have to tell me! Here, this thing, how does this thing**

1 work? *(He taps inside the engine with his wrench and looks*
2 *at the MOUNTAINEER expectantly.)*
3 MOUNTAINEER: Uhh...it's called the battery, your Holiness...
4 DALAI LAMA: Yes, I know what it's called, but how does it
5 *work*? You're from Europe, you should know.
6 MOUNTAINEER: Well...it's a sort of box, for storing energy...
7 DALAI LAMA: *(Impatiently)* I know what it does; *how does it*
8 *work*?
9 MOUNTAINEER: Well...inside it there are liquids...and certain
10 metals...they, uh, react...with each other...
11 DALAI LAMA: Yes? *(Pause)*
12 MOUNTAINEER: I don't know. Forgive me, your Holiness.
13 *(Pause. The DALAI LAMA reflects, then starts tinkering,*
14 *removing parts from the engine and laying them on the*
15 *fender.)*
16 DALAI LAMA: But...this machine is from your part of the
17 world, isn't it? How is it you don't understand?
18 MOUNTAINEER: *(Sighs.)* There are a lot of things I don't
19 understand, your Holiness.
20 DALAI LAMA: Really! Tell me another, maybe I can enlighten
21 you.
22 MOUNTAINEER: Well... *(He smiles slightly.)* I don't under-
23 stand war. Can you explain *that* to me?
24 DALAI LAMA: *(Tinkering)* You have wars often in your land?
25 In Austrr...
26 MOUNTAINEER: Austria. We have one right now, a terrible
27 war.
28 DALAI LAMA: I see. And what is the cause of this war?
29 MOUNTAINEER: A man named Hitler.
30 DALAI LAMA: One man! Why don't your people stop him?
31 MOUNTAINEER: He has too much power.
32 DALAI LAMA: But if he's just one man, he couldn't have as
33 much power as everyone else put together...
34 MOUNTAINEER: You'd think so, but millions of people do
35 just what he tells them to do.

1　DALAI LAMA: That doesn't make sense.
2　MOUNTAINEER: I know. You see, there are things in the
3　　　world that neither of us understands. Sometimes I feel
4　　　like I don't understand anything at all. *(Pause)* So I climb
5　　　mountains. I think to myself, maybe at the top of the
6　　　highest mountain, I'll find understanding.
7　DALAI LAMA: But you haven't found it there?
8　MOUNTAINEER: Not yet. *(Uncomfortably)* Your Holiness, I
9　　　came to Tibet to get away from the war. If I go back to
10　　　India, the British will lock me up, simply because I'm
11　　　Austrian. I need to stay away until the insanity in my
12　　　world has ended. *(The DALAI LAMA loosens a bolt with*
13　　　*his wrench.)*
14　DALAI LAMA: Then you might be here longer than you wish.
15　　　Insanity never ends, it merely changes form.
16　MOUNTAINEER: *(Hesitantly)* So...does that mean you'll allow
17　　　me to stay?
18　DALAI LAMA: *(Peers at him, brow furrowed.)* Of course. Why
19　　　not?
20　MOUNTAINEER: Your ministers want to throw me out of the
21　　　country; it's only because you wanted to meet me that
22　　　they've let me stay at all... *(The DALAI LAMA lifts the*
23　　　*battery out of the car. It is heavy; he struggles to hold it.)*
24　DALAI LAMA: Well, you know, they don't want anything to
25　　　invade our purity. *(He puts the battery down on the car's*
26　　　*fender.)* But tell me, doesn't *anyone* understand how this
27　　　battery-thing works? Or is it a mystery even to the people
28　　　that make it? *(The MOUNTAINEER thinks for a moment.)*
29　MOUNTAINEER: In my world, we understand less and less all
30　　　the time, rather than more. In fact, a few years ago, a
31　　　man named Einstein showed us that everything we had
32　　　thought about the universe was wrong. *(He taps the*
33　　　*battery matter-of-factly.)* He showed us that the energy in
34　　　this battery, and the metal box holding it, are merely two
35　　　different forms of the same thing. And also that things

only exist in relation to each other. Everything is connected. *(He smiles. The DALAI LAMA stares at him.)*
DALAI LAMA: But we Buddhists have known this for thou-
sands of years. *(He slams shut the hood of the car.)* I think
perhaps your world can also learn some things from mine.

Columbus Park

by Karen Huie

(Scene for a teenage Asian-American
boy and girl)

1   This delightful play is "a mosaic of Chinatown," as the play-
2 wright tells us. Jimmy and Chrissy are teenagers who have just
3 . returned to New York's Chinatown from a week's school vaca-
4 tion in Toronto. It's seven in the morning, the scene is Columbus
5 Park, and the couple has just stepped out of a car that has brought
6 them in from Toronto. They lug their suitcases and souvenirs
7 through the park. An elderly man is practicing Tai Chi, a Chinese
8 meditation form.
9
10   CHRISSY: What'd we come back here for?
11   JIMMY: We live here. You go to school today?
12   CHRISSY: We just got back!
13   JIMMY: You miss yesterday already.
14   CHRISSY: I'm too tired.
15   JIMMY: Then we go your house?
16   CHRISSY: My grandmother's still home.
17   JIMMY: We go there later when she go work.
18   CHRISSY: Maybe. Shit, I never sat in a car for seven hours! My
19   butt is buzzing. *(They sit on a bench.)*
20   JIMMY: What about me? You sleeping on the whole back
21   seat!
22   CHRISSY: Well, I didn't know!
23   JIMMY: And snore!
24   CHRISSY: I did not!
25   JIMMY: And talk!
26   CHRISSY: Get out!
27   JIMMY: *(Mimics.)* "Oh, make me feel so good!"
28   CHRISSY: You lie!
29   JIMMY: "More, I want —"
30   CHRISSY: Shut up! That guy'll hear you!
31   JIMMY: No, he do Tai Chi!
32   CHRISSY: My grandmother said he killed somebody.
33   JIMMY: He? Why?
34   CHRISSY: I don't know. After that he didn't talk to anyone
35   anymore.

1   JIMMY: What happened him?

2   CHRISSY: Don't know. Just stopped talking. God, the air's so

3   dirty here. Gray skies behind those buildings. Why is the

4   sky bluer in Toronto? Same sky, right? How come it's dif-

5   ferent over there? Jimmy? Jimmy! I asked you something!

6   What're you doing?

7   JIMMY: I not talk, just like that Tai Chi man.

8   CHRISSY: Very funny. *(Teasing)* Jimmy!

9   JIMMY: *(Teasing)* Chrissy!

10   CHRISSY: Let's go eat.

11   JIMMY: With this one? *(He indicates their luggage.)*

12   CHRISSY: Hey, you're wearing my shirt!

13   JIMMY: Of course, you buy for me.

14   CHRISSY: Yeah, cost me fifty bucks!

15   JIMMY: I like it.

16   CHRISSY: See? And you didn't like red. It is kind of loud now

17   that I look at it.

18   JIMMY: I wear because you buy for me.

19   CHRISSY: Awww. Jimmy?

20   JIMMY: Yeah?

21   CHRISSY: I miss the house with the dogs and chickens and –

22   what else was there? Oh yeah, ducks! Quack-quack-quack

23   – every morning at six, remember?

24   JIMMY: You not get up until ten!

25   CHRISSY: I could hear the ducks! Susie's auntie let me feed

26   them one morning! Saw me coming with the food and –

27   thought they were going to chew me to death! Let's get a

28   farm – with chickens and ducks and dogs!

29   JIMMY: Maybe after high school we go there. We lucky we get

30   the one week vacation.

31   CHRISSY: I know. I really like it there. I want to go back! How

32   about next week?

33   JIMMY: Okay, okay, we go next week. Maybe her auntie let us

34   stay her house little while.

35   CHRISSY: You think so?

1   JIMMY: Yeah. And I can get a job there and we have the family,
2   huh?
3   CHRISSY: Okay! Maybe your mother can take care of it for us!
4   I want one that looks like you.
5   JIMMY: Like you!
6   CHRISSY: You!
7   JIMMY: You! *(They kiss.)* Come one, we go your house and
8   make one now.
9   CHRISSY: Later! I'm hungry.
10   JIMMY: You always hungry! *(He pats CHRISSY's belly.)* Yeah,
11   much big now I be your boyfriend.
12   CHRISSY: You better pray that's food in there! Come on, let's
13   go eat. God, did Chinatown always stink this bad?
14   JIMMY: What we do with this? *(Indicates their luggage.)*
15   CHRISSY: Take it with us. Maybe they'll think we're tourists.
16   *(Pause)* Why don't they have crêpe suzettes in Chinatown?
17
18
19
20
21
22
23
24
25
26
27
28
29
30
31
32
33
34
35

The Ballad of Yachiyo

by Philip Kan Gotanda

(Scene for two Asian-American women)

1   This charming scene between Yachiyo and her friend Osugi
2   tracks two young Japanese-American teenagers as they come of
3   age in 1919 Hawaii. Osugi has a job cleaning up in the home of
4   rich Americans on the island of Kauai, and she has invited her
5   friend Yachiyo to spend the evening with her. As the Americans
6   dance and party inside the house, Osugi and Yachiyo are doing
7   chores in the kitchen area. Yachiyo has just dragged a bag of
8   garbage out, and re-enters the kitchen.
9
10   OSUGI: You lucky, yeah. You out of school, sit around the
11   house, a woman of leisure, huh.
12   YACHIYO: That's it? No more? *(YACHIYO starts to go back,*
13   *OSUGI catches her.)*
14   OSUGI: When the party's over we gotta clean up again.
15   Haole's so messy, yeah.
16   YACHIYO: There's some more stuff to throw out –
17   OSUGI: Yachiyo, no worry, okay. They'll still be dancing.
18   Pretty soon quiet down and then they start to hold each
19   other close.
20   YACHIYO: Then let's go watch, come on, Osugi. I wanna see
21   how the haoles – *(OSUGI has all the glasses lined up*
22   *neatly.)*
23   OSUGI: *(Interrupts.)* Sit, sit, I like to show you something. I
24   saw Mr. McDonald doing this. I thought it would be a
25   good lesson for you. Since you all the time interested in
26   what they wearing, how they dance. This is what they
27   drink. He had Alexander, the Plantation manager and
28   some of the lunas over for a meeting. Afterwards they did
29   this. A "tasting." I sneaked these out of his liquor cabinet.
30   *(OSUGI then pulls out a cigar.)* Cigar. It's important to
31   smoke cigars when you do this. That's what Mr.
32   McDonald say. *(Lights up cigar.)*
33   YACHIYO: Where you get dat?
34   OSUGI: The woman gave it to me. She hates the smell. Go
35   smoke 'em. Smoke 'em all up, she tell me. She gave me a

1   whole bag full. All the way from Europe. Mr. McDonald
2   find out he hit the roof. I gave some of them to Pantat to
3   give to his worker friends. Here.
4   YACHIYO: No.
5   OSUGI: Take, take. Don't inhale, just puff. *(Curiosity gets the*
6   *better of YACHIYO, and she takes it and puffs it. They con-*
7   *tinue to pass it back and forth. YACHIYO grows more*
8   *emboldened in her smoking style.)* Mr. McDonald almost
9   caught Pantat. He ride up on his fine horse and catch
10   Pantat taking one pee break and smoking one of his
11   cigars. "Oh, hi, Mr. Boss. This is one big cigar, you like try
12   one?" Mr. McDonald don't know which cigar Pantat is
13   talking about. He just grunts and rides away. Pantat, I
14   like crack him over the head if he lose his job. Okay, okay,
15   now this one here is... *(She pulls out a crumpled piece of*
16   *paper and reads.)* ...Jamesons.
17   YACHIYO: *(Puffing)* What's that?
18   OSUGI: Irish Whiskey. This is "Courvosier," a "cog-nac." *(She*
19   *has a hard time pronouncing.)* This is a coffee liqueur.
20   And this is my favorite, champagne. I love this one. It's so
21   good. See the bubbles. I know you like it so I got a bottle.
22   *(Takes a swig.)* Mmmm, all the bubbles.
23   YACHIYO: Osugi, you gonna get into trouble.
24   OSUGI: Hey, I get you a job here. Da other girl, Shimokawa,
25   getting big, starting to show, they fire her as soon as they
26   know.
27   YACHIYO: I don't know, things at the house. You know, the
28   kids, Mama's overworked –
29   OSUGI: *(Handing YACHIYO the bottle, taking the cigar)* You
30   outta school now, you can't sit on your butt around the
31   house. Besides your papa not working, let him help out
32   around dere. Dis is a good job, not have to get all hot and
33   stinky like –
34   YACHIYO: *(Sips, overlapping)* Mmmm, this is good...
35   OSUGI: – in the cane field. Clean house, throw out the

1   garbage, help in the kitchen, you get to eat the food, too,
2   if they don't catch you... *(YACHIYO starts to take another*
3   *drink.)* Hey, hey, enough already. You trying to ruin your
4   taste buds? Start from here. Try dat. *(YACHIYO hesitantly*
5   *sips the cognac. OSUGI, puffing, watches her intently.)*
6   YACHIYO: Strong, I think it's good. I can't tell.
7   OSUGI: It's French. Try dis one.
8   YACHIYO: *(Sipping)* Mmmm. This is good. Just like coffee and
9   candy at same time. I like this.
10 OSUGI: McDonald Okusan likes this. Mr. McDonald, he don't
11   like it. He likes this one. *(YACHIYO takes a big gulp of the*
12   *Jamesons.)*
13 YACHIYO: *(Spits it out.)* What's that?
14 OSUGI: Hey, don't waste, very expensive whiskey. I drink if
15   you don't like. *(OSUGI gulps it down.)*
16 YACHIYO: You like dat?
17 OSUGI: *(Making a face)* No, but if it's expensive I drink it —
18   *(With fake haole accent)* — "even if it tastes like caca."
19   Okay, now we try the champagne again. *(OSUGI takes an*
20   *enthusiastic swig and passes it to YACHIYO.)* All bubbly,
21   huh, make your head spin. Later we have some cake, too.
22   See how clean and bubbly it taste. Not all sweet like that
23   cheap pake stuff my step-papa drinks when he plays
24   mah-jong —
25 YACHIYO: Osugi? Osugi, show me how they dance.
26 OSUGI: I'm drinking, drinking...
27 YACHIYO: *(Dragging OSUGI to her feet)* Come on, come on,
28   enough drinking — show me how they do it.
29 OSUGI: *(Putting bottle down)* You should get Willie to dance
30   with you. *(Music volume rises, an up-tempo song. OSUGI*
31   *and YACHIYO start to dance. OSUGI has to guide YACHIYO,*
32   *pushing her along. It's a fun and lively rendition.)* Drink
33   break, drink break...
34 YACHIYO: No, no, come on, Osugi, show me the slow one now.
35   Show me the slow one. *(OSUGI grabs the champagne*

1   *bottle as YACHIYO pulls her back. OSUGI pulls YACHIYO*
2   *close. Music changes to a slow tempo.)*
3   **OSUGI:** Like dis.
4   **YACHIYO:** Like dis?
5   **OSUGI:** *(Drinking from bottle)* Yeah. Just like dis.
6   **YACHIYO:** So close, yeah? The boy's body pushed up close
7   like dis?
8   **OSUGI:** Haole's dance nasty, yeah.
9   **YACHIYO:** *(Stopping)* That's enough.
10   **OSUGI:** What? You and Willie don't do this kind of thing?
11   **YACHIYO:** I'm thirsty. *(YACHIYO takes the bottle and takes a*
12   *big gulp.)*
13   **OSUGI:** Pantat and me, all the time do this kind of thing. Not
14   dancing, but you know.
15   **YACHIYO:** We don't do that kind of thing.
16   **OSUGI:** How come – Willie's cute, yeah?
17   **YACHIYO:** That kind of thing get you into trouble, Osugi.
18   **OSUGI:** Sometimes you so old-fashioned, Yachiyo. Everybody
19   does it some.
20   **YACHIYO:** Do that kind of thing you end up bringing shame
21   to your family. Then you have nothing, no family,
22   nothing. End up like that Shimokawa girl.
23   **OSUGI:** *(During the following, YACHIYO moves away.)* Shim-
24   okawa, she's a stupid girl, go too far. Go so far, cannot
25   come back. And now, she don't even have no boyfriend to
26   take care of the baby. I've got Pantat. He always take care
27   of me. Just like Willie. He always take care you, Yachiyo.
28   He dance good, too. Don't listen to your parents. They're
29   only interested in what makes them happy, not you. You
30   gonna end up an old maid, working for those old farts
31   down in Waimea.
32
33
34
35

Yellow Fever

by Rick A. Shiomi

(Scene for an Asian-American man and woman)

1   Sam Shikaze is a Japanese-Canadian private eye from the
2   Sam Spade school of life who lives and works on Powell Street in
3   Vancouver. While working on a missing person case, he and
4   Nancy Wing, a young reporter from the local newspaper, strike
5   up a relationship. The romantic comedy of the following scene is
6   typical of the tongue-in-cheek style of the rest of the play, which
7   relies on stereotypes of the men, women, tough detectives and
8   shameless villains who peopled the Hollywood detective movies
9   of the forties.

10

11   **SAM: Things are coming together, eh, kid?**
12   **NANCY: Look, I'm not a kid. Maybe I am new at the business,**
13   **and I've made my share of mistakes, but I've figured**
14   **some things out for myself.**
15   **SAM: Yeah, you've come a long way.**
16   **NANCY:** *(Pause)* **I never thought I'd hear that from you...**
17   **SAM: You're doing all right.**
18   **NANCY:** *(Walking toward SAM)* **I feel like I've touched a soft**
19   **spot in the bedrock.**
20   **SAM: Why don't we just stick to the story, you know, keep it**
21   **simple.**
22   **NANCY: I didn't mean to distract you...but you don't ever take**
23   **time off? Just to relax and talk about things...or even**
24   **watch TV?**
25   **SAM: Yeah, at home.**
26   **NANCY: But you're never there.**
27   **SAM: Okay, Nancy, what's on your mind?**
28   **NANCY:** *(Walking away)* **Jesus, Sam, do you have to be so**
29   **abrupt? Is everything so cut and dry for you?**
30   **SAM:** *(Pause)* **My wife said I'd dried up, that living with me**
31   **was like dying of thirst in the desert.**
32   **NANCY: She didn't pull any punches, did she?**
33   **SAM: I heard a lot worse.**
34   **NANCY: But it doesn't have to be that way.**
35   **SAM: No, it didn't.**

1 NANCY: I mean you care about people, like Rosie and Chuck.

2 SAM: That's different.

3 NANCY: It's only another way of caring. Maybe it wasn't your

4   fault. Maybe it was the relationship, or your wife.

5 SAM: She had problems all right, but I was the biggest one.

6   She wanted to entertain friends, and take long vacations,

7   have a big house in Shaughnessy with me playing the

8   breadwinner. She had plans to turn me into a somebody.

9 NANCY: I've talked to plenty of people around here, and they

10   all look up to you. Not those stuff-shirt nisei hiding out

11   in the suburbs, but the people who live around here.

12   You can't measure that in dollars and cents. Your wife

13   couldn't understand what you were doing!

14 SAM: So what are you getting worked up about?

15 NANCY: I don't know.

16 SAM: What'd I do now?

17 NANCY: Nothing...that's the problem. Don't you feel anything

18   through that thick skin of yours?

19 SAM: Yeah, I've been here before.... I got a knack for upsetting

20   women.

21 NANCY: Jesus Christ!

22 SAM: Look, Nancy, you're an attractive young woman.

23 NANCY: You sound like somebody's uncle.... Sam...I care

24   about you.

25 SAM: *(Pause)* Yeah. *(Pause)* I could see you comin' a mile away.

26   You were so busy winding yourself up for the big

27   romance that you forgot one thing: you don't know me

28   from nobody. To you I'm somebody who looks good in a

29   back alley when you're scared. You want a hero but

30   you're just setting yourself up for the fall.

31 NANCY: That's my business, Sam. You think you're the first

32   guy in my life? I've been around and I can take care of

33   myself. Maybe I am looking for a hero, somebody with

34   character.... Who the hell isn't!

35 SAM: That makes great copy, kid, but what else have I got? A

1   one-room walkup with no closet space? You want to
2   listen to music on a beat-up old radio? Make out on a
3   lumpy mattress? You think we got a chance of lastin' five
4   minutes beyond this case?
5   NANCY: It doesn't matter. I've got my own career and space.
6   We don't have to live together.
7   SAM: You're the liberated type, eh?
8   NANCY: Does it have to be love and marriage, or love 'em and
9   leave 'em? Isn't there room in your life for a mature rela-
10   tionship between consenting adults?
11 SAM: That was a mouthful, kid, and maybe that's your style,
12   but I got my own way of doin' things.
13 NANCY: I can see that, but isn't there any room for the two of
14   us to share?
15 SAM: Give me a breather, kid, we gotta think about this first.
16 NANCY: At least you're talking "we" now.
17 SAM: Why me? You could have your pick of the hotshots down-
18   town. Chuck could go for you, and he's more your age.
19 NANCY: I'm looking for someone older, someone who's been
20   around, knows the score the way you do.
21 SAM: What do you want, a father?
22 NANCY: That's not what I had in mind.
23 SAM: I'm getting nervous, kid.
24 NANCY: I mean it. You don't want or need the things most
25   guys do to feel good about themselves. You don't need a
26   flashy car or a new office or fancy women to stroke your
27   ego. You don't need things to protect you from the world
28   out there. You're different, you're weird.... You're down
29   here on Powell Street because you want to be, you're not
30   hiding out, you're just living here, like somebody who
31   doesn't care if the world passes him by, because the
32   world isn't going anywhere!
33 SAM: Who would've believed this, eh? An old guy like me
34   makin' time with someone like you.
35 NANCY: Sam, I'm gonna scream if you call yourself old again.

1   You're in the prime of your life.

2   SAM: Maybe I'd rather not think about that.

3   NANCY: Why not?

4   SAM: *(Pause)* 'Cause you start lookin' over your shoulder at
5   how easy it used to be. You turn forty and you're still
6   alone, and suddenly the old hot plate doesn't heat up
7   enough to boil water. You get up and stare at the walls
8   around you and wonder what's the use. You want to
9   know why I spend all my time here? 'Cause this is where
10   I live, this is what I call home.... This is all I got!

11   NANCY: Sam...

12   SAM: You want to know where these bruises came from? A
13   couple of goons jumped me, right here in my own god-
14   damned office! Twenty years ago I would have wiped the
15   floor with their asses...and last night they kicked mine.
16   *(Pause)* The prime of life? Who're you kidding? It's the
17   edge, and when you look out there it's dark, and fear
18   turns your insides.

19   NANCY: But you don't change. You just go on.

20   SAM: You're too young to understand.

21   NANCY: You're not afraid of growing old alone. You're afraid of
22   me, afraid of having to wake up and feel again. You want to
23   go out like some dirty old butt! Look at you, look at this
24   place! You've grown comfortable here, surrounded by
25   "The Community," by Mrs. Tanaka and her crazy son, by
26   old man Shimizu and his lost wallets, by Mr. Kudo and his
27   missing daughter. You look at me and all you see is trouble,
28   somebody who doesn't fit into your little world!

29   SAM: What the hell do you want?

30   NANCY: You! The guy that calls his own shots.

31   SAM: *(Pause)* I don't know, it's been a long time. *(NANCY walks*
32   *up behind him.)*

33   NANCY: Not that long. *(Pause)* You know, you're pretty good-
34   looking when you get going. *(SAM reaches out and pulls*
35   *NANCY to him.)*

1   SAM: You don't let up...do you? *(They kiss.)*

2   NANCY: I like to think I get my man.

3   SAM: You and the Mounted Police, eh?

4   NANCY: They got nothing on me.

5   SAM: Well, you just about got this one.

6   NANCY: That's not good enough.

7   SAM: All right, I give up.... *(They kiss again.)*

8

9

10

11

12

13

14

15

16

17

18

19

20

21

22

23

24

25

26

27

28

29

30

31

32

33

34

35

Struggling Truths

by Peter Mellencamp

(Scene for an Asian man and woman)

1   This play portrays the emerging situation of Tibet in the
2 modern world by contrasting the values of western European
3 and Chinese societies with those of Tibet. In this early scene,
4 Dorje and his older sister, Rinchen, are talking of their bleak
5 future: Rinchen wishes to remain on their family's farm and
6 work it, while Dorje aspires to travel to the capitol city, Lhasa,
7 where he can study philosophy with the lamas. Dorje is pros-
8 trating himself (pressing his hands together and touching them
9 to his forehead, throat and chest, then kneeling and pressing his
10 forehead to the ground), and performing prayers as the scene
11 opens; his sister is nearby, sharpening knives.
12
13 RINCHEN: **It's been three months.**
14 DORJE: *(In the midst of his prayers)* **I know.**
15 RINCHEN: **Dorje, Mom and Dad were getting older; we all**
16   **have to die sometime.**
17 DORJE: **No. You die for a reason. Because you starve, or you**
18   **have an accident, or you get sick, or *something*. You don't**
19   **just drop dead out in the fields one day.**
20 RINCHEN: **Dorje, we have to go on with life —**
21 DORJE: **Get on with my life? What *is* my life? Is this all it**
22   **comes down to, one day falling over in the middle of a**
23   **field? It just doesn't make sense! Don't you ever think**
24   **about that?**
25 RINCHEN: ***I don't have time!* I'm doing twice as much work**
26   **now that they're dead.... And it'll be twice as much again,**
27   **if you leave.**
28 DORJE: **I *am* leaving. I've decided.** *(Pause)*
29 RINCHEN: **When?**
30 DORJE: **Tomorrow.**
31 RINCHEN: **I see.** *(Pause)* **Well then...that's that.** *(She looks off*
32   *in the distance. DORJE looks at her out of the corner of his*
33   *eye. Pause)*
34 DORJE: **I saw you this morning, down by the river with**
35   **Thubten.**

176

1   RINCHEN: So? I can spend a few minutes with him if I want...!

2   DORJE: You were riding on that wagon thing his father built.

3   RINCHEN: So?! Listen, his back was sore, I was just giving

4   him a massage, that's *all* –

5   DORJE: Rinchen, that wagon has *wheels*. *(RINCHEN groans.)*

6   You know the prophecy –

7   DORJE & RINCHEN: "With the wheel comes the End" –

8   RINCHEN: – I know, I know –

9   DORJE: So stay away from them, they're dangerous!

10 RINCHEN: Dorje, with those "dangerous wheels," Thubten's

11   family grows five times as much as we do!

12 DORJE: That is *not* the reason. *(Pause)* Thubten's father must

13   have given a lot of money to the lamas when he went to

14   Lhasa last year. Or else it's merit he brought with him

15   from his past lives, anyway, it's not his wheeled things,

16   don't be a fool.

17 RINCHEN: Well, after you're gone I'm going to build one.

18 DORJE: Rinchen, no –!

19 RINCHEN: Well, what if after you leave I can't pay the taxes?

20   I'll have to go into debt to Thubten's father, and you *know*

21   what a bastard he is! If I make the wheels –

22 DORJE: Oh, fine, let's just dump all the traditions, throw away

23   everything that makes us what we are –

24 RINCHEN: Right. Starving, diseased –

25 DORJE: *No! Peaceful and compassionate!* ...Now look what

26   you've done, you made me lose count! *(He starts counting*

27   *his prayers again. RINCHEN rushes to DORJE and starts*

28   *tickling him.)*

29 RINCHEN: My sweet little brother.... *Why* do you have to go to

30   Lhasa, can't you just study at the monastery here?

31 DORJE: You *know* why! The Grand Lama *here* cares more

32   about collecting taxes than he does about teaching, and

33   he beats his disciples! Why do you think they look so

34   unhappy!

35 RINCHEN: You told me it's because they're contemplating the

1   fact that all life is suffering.

2   DORJE: All life in *that* place, that's for sure. *(RINCHEN pushes*

3   *him angrily and moves away, going back to her knives.)*

4   RINCHEN: All right then go, see if I care. I'll just stay here and

5   die of exhaustion before I'm thirty.... Or maybe I'll marry

6   Thubten and his brother, they'd make a nice pair of

7   husbands.

8   DORJE: Oh, God, no! Thubten maybe, but not *Drugpa*! He's a

9   *pig*!

10   RINCHEN: Aw, is poor little Dorje still hurting from when big

11   bad Drugpa pushed him in the river?

12   DORJE: Pushed?! He *hit* me, he almost broke my nose! I *hate*

13   him, he's a piece of yak dung, I hope he dies tomorrow

14   and gets reincarnated as a bug so I can squash him...!

15   *(Catching himself)* There, you see? *That's* why I have to

16   study with the lamas, this *anger* keeps coming up inside

17   me....

18   RINCHEN: I get angry all the time, so what? Dorje —

19   DORJE: So I hate it! I want the peace I used to have, I want to

20   feel the Buddha's infinite compassion, even toward a

21   piece of shit like Drugpa. *(DORJE jumps up and deter-*

22   *minedly begins doing prostrations again.)* There's an

23   emptiness inside me, and it's killing me. And the

24   monastery in Lhasa is the only place I know of where I

25   might be able to fill it.

26   RINCHEN: *(Sharpening a knife, not looking at DORJE)* All right,

27   then go.... But when you're there, think about me, *here*,

28   working to pay the lamas' taxes so you can sit with them

29   and talk philosophy. *(DORJE pauses, his hands pressed*

30   *together at his heart.)*

31   DORJE: I will always think of you.

32

33

34

35

Baby Jesus

by Issac Bedonna

(Scene for one Hispanic and
one Asian-American boy)

1   Two twelve-year-old boys are hiding in their secret fort:
2   Marlon Ota, an Asian-American, and his friend Berto Ochoa, a
3   Mexican-American. Their excited discussion revolves around the
4   fact that the Ota family may be moving away soon, and the
5   friendship between Marlon and Berto will be threatened. The
6   fort is the crawlspace beneath the floor of the Ochoa house in
7   suburban Los Angeles. It is very dark, and both boys carry flash-
8   lights. Marlon is coughing.
9
10   **BERTO: Should be finishing my science project, Marlon.**
11   **MARLON: Here's my *last* official visit to the clubhouse.**
12   **BERTO: I know. Your asthma.**
13   **MARLON: Wow, I'll never get over it.** *(He shines his flashlight*
14   *along the wall.)*
15   **BERTO: What?**
16   **MARLON: The only walls on your block *not* covered with graf-**
17   **fiti are under your house!**
18   **BERTO:** *(Shining his light in MARLON's face. Meaning*
19   *"untrue")* **Uh-huh!**
20   **MARLON:** *(Blinded)* **Don't!** *(Pushing the light away)* **Okay!**
21   **Special meeting for two reasons.** *(Pulling a white bag out*
22   *of his jacket pocket)* **First — mmm, pork buns!**
23   **BERTO: Yay! "Cha Shu Bao!"**
24   **MARLON:** *(Sharing the bag with BERTO, chuckling)* **"Aye, que**
25   **bueno!"** *(Both boys giggle over exchanging languages*
26   *again.)* **The second reason, Berto. Your grandmother,**
27   ***when* will you tell her? "*Cuando*?!"**
28   **BERTO:** *Sshhh!* *(Pointing upward)* **They'll hear! Mom'll**
29   **punish me if she finds out about this fort.**
30   **MARLON: Tough Kabuki!** *(BERTO holds finger to his lips for*
31   *"quiet.")* ***Two months ago* you were supposed to tell her!**
32   **BERTO: Your loud mouth, Marlon! If I go to bed early, no**
33   **finding out what's in that box upstairs.**
34   **MARLON: It's from Josephina's mother *who was a nun*?**
35   **BERTO: Grandma's sister, Graciella, entered the convent**

1   when Josey was probably our age.

2   MARLON: Your grandmother baby-sits Josephina ever since?

3   Then the lady who just died. Who —

4   BERTO: Consuelo. Grandma's aunt. But Consuelo wound up

5   raising my grandma —

6   MARLON: Just like your grandmother raising you. *No fair*!

7   Changing subjects! *(Shining his flashlight in BERTO's face)*

8   Berto, my father knows people in high places, but dead-

9   lines are deadlines.

10   BERTO: *(Pushed) Okay*!

11   MARLON: Our new school needs registration forms filled out

12   *now*!

13   BERTO: *Shhh*!

14   MARLON: Get with the program, "amigo." Pronto! Because

15   this summer the Ota family moves up North *(Pointing

16   upward)* with or without Berto Ochoa!

17

18

19

20

21

22

23

24

25

26

27

28

29

30

31

32

33

34

35

Songs of Harmony

by Karen Huie

(Scene for two Asian-American sisters)

1   This amusing scene is set in the home of middle-class
2 Chinese immigrants, where the two American-born daughters,
3 Emily and her younger sister Suzanne, are busily trying to bring
4 some order to the chaos of their family surroundings. Suzanne,
5 a tense, born-again Christian, is ready to strangle her husband
6 and his girlfriend for wrecking her marriage; Emily, a graphic
7 designer who has always lived at home, is trying to figure out
8 what she'll need to take with her in order to live with her
9 boyfriend; and meanwhile the oldest sister, Elaine, is about to
10 arrive home after ditching her marriage to become a pop singer.
11 The locale is Emily's bedroom, where Suzanne is helping her
12 pack. At rise, the phone rings, and Emily answers it.
13
14 EMILY: *(Into phone)* **Hello...? Yes, this is.... Well, she's landed**
15   **but she's not....Mitchell? Oh, Michio.** *(Pause)* **Ya-Ma-**
16   *Gotcha. (Pause)* **Yama***guchi***, that's what I said! Okay, I'll**
17   **tell her. Bye.** *(To SUZANNE)* **Why isn't he coming? You two**
18   **were gonna spend the night and help move my stuff out**
19   **tomorrow morning!**
20 SUZANNE: **Do it yourself!**
21 EMILY: **Myself? Why doesn't he want to help me? What**
22   **happened?**
23 SUZANNE: **Nothing.** *(Pause)* **We had a fight.**
24 EMILY: **Again? Now what?**
25 SUZANNE: **Nothing...never mind. Couples have fights, you**
26   **know! Lots of 'em!**
27 EMILY: **Why, 'cause he wouldn't help with the dishes?**
28 SUZANNE: **Don't be stupid! I never ask for help with the**
29   **dishes!**
30 EMILY: **Well then, why'd you bring your suitcase?**
31 SUZANNE: **I haven't seen Elaine in two years! Can't I come**
32   **spend the night with my sister?**
33 EMILY: **Sisters, Suzanne, you have two!**
34 SUZANNE: **Yeah, well, you're always here!**
35 EMILY: **Sure! The one who stays always gets taken for**

1   granted! Well, I'm not gonna hang around anymore for
2   you guys to –
3   SUZANNE: Aren't you finished packing yet?
4   EMILY: No, thanks to you!
5   SUZANNE: Don't start with me! You're lucky I'm here! *(Looks*
6   *around.)* Look at this place! It's a mess! What've you
7   packed so far?
8   EMILY: Well, I put all my mechanical pencils in here, with my
9   art supplies. Everything that goes on my drafting table is
10   in a separate box so they'll – be in one box. Oh, Suzanne!
11   Wait till you see my –
12   SUZANNE: Mechanical pencils? Art supplies? What about
13   *clothes*, and *linen* and *towels*?
14   EMILY: Well, I don't know what to take. I've never done this
15   before. Maybe he'll bring them.
16   SUZANNE: You can't depend on men to think of these things!
17   EMILY: Shared responsibilities, Suzanne! Sometimes I do the
18   dishes, sometimes he does them. That's how it's going
19   to be.
20   SUZANNE: Sure it is! *(Pause)* You'd better make a list of every-
21   thing! Think about all the things you use, starting from
22   in the morning until night. *(Pause)* Forget it, you're
23   moving tomorrow! Look, this is what you do... *(SUZANNE*
24   *lies on the bed.)* ...You're sleeping, okay? You get up!
25   What's the first thing you do?
26   EMILY: I pee.
27   SUZANNE: You look at your alarm clock! *(SUZANNE grabs the*
28   *clock and throws it into a box.)* What do you do next?
29   EMILY: Next? Ummm...I shut it off!
30   SUZANNE: After that!
31   EMILY: I pee. *(SUZANNE gathers up the cover in a huff and*
32   *throws it into another box.)* I gotta pee. *(EMILY heads for*
33   *the door. SUZANNE grabs and pushes EMILY onto the bed*
34   *to continue the process.)* I don't know, Suzanne, it's kind
35   of flowery, don't you think?

1   SUZANNE: If he doesn't like it, that's just too bad! Let him
2   sleep on the floor! He's lucky you wash and change the
3   sheets every week for him!
4   EMILY: I do?
5   SUZANNE: You can throw it out when you get a new one.
6   EMILY: Throw it out? Mom made this for me! *(Pause)* I'll leave
7   it here for Elaine.
8   SUZANNE: Elaine? She's just comin' in for an audition, isn't
9   she? I can't believe she gave up her marriage to become a
10   singer. *(EMILY lies down again on the bed, mimes flipping*
11   *the imaginary cover, sits up and puts on her slippers. She*
12   *throws the slippers into another box. EMILY goes through*
13   *the rising ritual again, sees her robe and tosses it into*
14   *another box.)*
15   EMILY: You gave up the violin to become a Southern Baptist!
16   Same thing, isn't it? Went to that Christian college in
17   Louisiana!
18   SUZANNE: Ugh! How can you compare the mission of God
19   with a career?
20   EMILY: You know what I mean. What're you so touchy about?
21   SUZANNE: You! You call yourself a Christian? As far as I'm
22   concerned, you're only a carnal Christian! You shouldn't
23   even be moving in with Andrew. Living together is
24   wrong, you know.
25   EMILY: Oh, brother! What is with you?
26   SUZANNE: But if that's what you want, fine! *(SUZANNE*
27   *storms out.)*
28   EMILY: Isn't that what I'm supposed to do?
29   SUZANNE: *I'll help you move out!* *(SUZANNE returns with an*
30   *armful of towels.)*
31   EMILY: What're you doing? You can't take these! Don't you
32   think everyone'll notice they're missing? All right, maybe
33   two, one for me and one for him.
34   SUZANNE: Two towels for two people?
35   EMILY: We haven't discussed it yet. *(SUZANNE frantically folds*

1   *the towels and throws them into EMILY's boxes.)*

2   SUZANNE: I give Christopher a fresh set of towels every day!

3   That's *three* towels a day: a bath towel, a hand towel and

4   a face cloth. Every day Times seven! Twenty-one towels

5   for him alone — a week! Butterscotch on Sundays, robin

6   blue on Mondays —

7   EMILY: Twenty-one towels? Suzanne, we never needed a

8   fresh set of towels every day! Once a week, that's all!

9   SUZANNE: I even make him a different dessert every night

10   from scratch! Lemon parfait on Tuesdays, Cannolies,

11   Anise toast on —

12   EMILY: Anise toast?

13   SUZANNE: They're delicious! That rat!

14   EMILY: Who says the guy has to have a special desert every

15   night? Buy him a tub of ice cream! Let the guy feed

16   himself!

17   SUZANNE: I'll bet she doesn't do that?

18   EMILY: Who?

19   SUZANNE: Her!

20   EMILY: Her?

21   SUZANNE: Shut up!

22   EMILY: What?

23   SUZANNE: Shut up!

24   EMILY: Okay! *(EMILY is stunned. SUZANNE cries.)*

25   SUZANNE: What's she got that I haven't got? *(Pause)* I'm a

26   good wife! "Keeper of the house," just like the Bible says.

27   EMILY: Wait a minute! Christopher? With another —? Who?

28   SUZANNE: I'll kill him!

29   EMILY: That hypocrite! Praise the Lord, huh? Got Jesus to

30   guide you, huh? Kill him!

31   SUZANNE: We took a vow!

32   EMILY: Here, take my X-acto knife!

33   SUZANNE: I was there every night when he came home.

34   Elaine's husband had something to complain about. She

35   was always at a rehearsal or singing somewhere. I gave

1   up trying to be a concert violinist for God and the church

2   and my marriage! Emily, what am I gonna do?

3   EMILY: Kill him!

4   SUZANNE: I can't.

5   EMILY: Well, castrate him, at least!

6   SUZANNE: I'll kill her!

7   EMILY: Better get Mom's cleaver for that! See? It pays to be

8   selfish, just like Mom says. *(Beat)* Look, Suzanne, he

9   didn't deserve you. The guy's a schlemiel, let's face it!

10   And I'm sorry, Suzanne, but those bushy blonde eye-

11   brows – and body odor! No offense, Suzanne, but you're

12   starting to smell like him, too!

13   SUZANNE: He can't help it if he smells!

14   EMILY: Well, I can't help it if I can smell him!

15   SUZANNE: We'd better go help Mom before she has a fit.

16   EMILY: Me? You're the one who's supposed to come at four!

17   SUZANNE: Don't tell me! I don't see you down there setting up!

18   EMILY: All right, all right! Don't say anything to her yet, okay?

19   Just let me finish packing.

20   SUZANNE: That could take forever! *(SUZANNE exits. EMILY*

21   *looks around, overwhelmed.)*

22

23

24

25

26

27

28

29

30

31

32

33

34

35

Tokyo Carmen Versus L. A. Carmen

by Karen Tei Yamashita

(Scene for two couples, one
Asian and one Caucasian)

1   This presentational-type scene is taken from a play de-
2 signed for multimedia sound effects and projections, dance and
3 music. The drama contrasts the lifestyles in Japan and the
4 United States by following the lives of two family groups: Jiro
5 and his wife Maki, and Jiro's mother, who live in Torrance where
6 Jiro works for a Japanese firm; and Joe and his wife Michelle,
7 with Joe's mother, who live in a Tokyo suburb where Joe is a self-
8 employed businessman. The formal positioning and dialog of
9 the four characters in this scene (Jiro, Joe, Maki and Michelle),
10 reveal their backgrounds, feelings and hopes for the future in a
11 startlingly theatrical manner.
12
13 *I/Micaela*
14 MAKI: I came with my husband Jiro and my mother-in-law to
15   live in L.A. My husband said it is his duty to sell as many
16   cars in America as possible; otherwise, he will be
17   demoted and return to Japan dishonorably.
18 MICHELLE: I came with my husband Joe and my mother-in-
19   law to live in Tokyo. Back in L.A., my husband was a
20   respectable car salesman. Now he's a soldier in the trade
21   war. We've come to Tokyo to infiltrate the market.
22 MAKI: My husband Jiro works very hard. I never see him
23   anymore.
24 MICHELLE: This business of Joe's is really innovative. He's
25   selling ground meat to the Japanese in vending
26   machines. My Joe says it is his patriotic duty to sell as
27   many meat vending machines in Japan as possible.
28 MAKI: All day, I am in this big American house in Torrance. I
29   should be grateful. There are four bedrooms and three
30   bathrooms and a big living room, big kitchen, big
31   washing machine, big dishwasher and giant refrigerator.
32   There is a TV in every room. I have a big American car to
33   go to giant supermarket. I should be very happy.
34 MICHELLE: I never thought I'd ever be living in such an itty-
35   bitty house; everywhere you turn, you bump into

1   something. The bathroom is so small you can only take a
2   bath if you close this door, but you can't use the toilet
3   unless you open the door. I'm getting this claustrophobia
4   thing where I think the walls of my mind are closing in
5   on me. You can't get away from it even when you step
6   outside. Out there, it's wall-to-wall Japanese.
7   MAKI: My mother-in-law is very sick, but she made the sacri-
8   fice for Jiro to come to L.A. I try to make her happy by
9   feeding her Japanese food, but she doesn't talk so much.
10   She is watching Japanese TV, channel eighteen or fifty-
11   six or sleeping all day. I cannot leave her alone, so I am
12   watching TV all day, too.
13   MICHELLE: Joe's mom made the trip with us. She was a real
14   trooper till she got here, fell, broke her hip and got laid
15   up. I do my best to keep her happy, but I'm having a heck
16   of a time finding anything she'd like to eat. Lately, she
17   doesn't talk much. All day long she stares at the TV; can't
18   understand a word; just stares.
19   MAKI: I am also sometimes practicing my tea ceremony
20   which I learned before I got married. I don't want to
21   forget in case we go back to Japan.
22   MICHELLE: I been trying to learn Japanese from watching
23   American programs on TV, but I'm not getting anywhere
24   fast. It's all dubbed. I don't know why they do that; the
25   Japanese could be learning English.
26   MAKI: It is my greatest dream to return to Japan to become
27   education mama.
28   MICHELLE: It's my ideal to become a working mother.
29   MAKI: I wish to have a boy to nurse and feed...
30   MICHELLE: I wanna take maternity leave to have a boy...
31   MAKI: ...and when he goes to school to send him off every
32   morning with a good meal...
33   MICHELLE: ...then I wanna work full-time and leave him at
34   the sitters and day care...
35   MAKI: ...and then to pick him up from school and to take him

1   to English lessons, piano lessons, tennis lessons, math
2   lessons, swimming lessons...
3 MICHELLE: ...and be able to rush out of my job on the excuse
4   that my son has a doctor's appointment or that I should
5   attend a PTA meeting or to hear him play the cymbals in
6   the school orchestra.
7 MAKI: ...to violin lessons, judo, baseball, to help him with all
8   his homework, and to follow him every step of the way to
9   ensure his success in life and to urge him on to study to
10   enter a famous university.
11 MICHELLE: I would rush home every day from work to cook
12   his favorite dinner – macaroni and cheese, play a game
13   of Nintendo, help him with his homework, get him in
14   and out of his bath, read him a story, in short, give
15   quality time every evening of his childhood life.
16 MAKI: Well, we came to L.A. We are lonely, but Jiro works too
17   hard to notice. At first I call my mother on the phone all
18   the time, but I have nothing new to tell her. I got lonely
19   hearing about home and my old friends all having
20   babies, all becoming education mama.
21 MICHELLE: Well, I gotta put that working mother plan on a
22   back burner till we get back to L.A. This place is too
23   small. No family room. No big back yard with grass to cut
24   and a swing set. How're you supposed to raise kids like
25   this? I'll be lucky to fit a bassinet in here.
26 MAKI: I felt sad. Jiro's mother doesn't say much; there is no
27   one to talk to. I begin to forget how to talk.
28 MICHELLE: I tell Joe I'm not getting any younger, but he's too
29   busy fighting the trade war. When he comes home, he
30   practically slumps over and snores right there in the
31   door with the shoes. And we got no privacy. You got no
32   incentive with your mother-in-law right over there on
33   the other side of the rice paper.
34 MAKI: I go to doctor. The doctor says nothing wrong with me.
35   Nothing wrong with Jiro. Just we got to be patient, got to

1   relax. Maybe we got to have sex, too.

2   MICHELLE: I get letters from home saying so-and-so had a

3   baby or got pregnant, and I get really depressed. All I'm

4   doing is counting the days till this trade war is over.

5   MAKI: Jiro only comes home to sleep. The doctor says we got

6   to get a vacation, see America, enjoy life. Jiro is too busy.

7   Work is first. Play later. Jiro doesn't want to have baby in

8   America; then baby will be American, lose Japanese

9   ways, be weak in competition, lose trade war. I am

10   waiting every day for war to end, go back to Japan, have

11   my baby and raise my son.

12   * * *

13   *II/Dragoons*

14   JIRO: I have been with the company since I graduated Keio

15   University. I have been promoted every year and moving

16   up the company. Finally I was sent to the L.A. office. This

17   was a big opportunity and responsibility for me, to be

18   sent to the front.

19   JOE: I got into exporting ground meat to Japan because I

20   figure I ought to do something for my country. Before, I

21   had it real good, selling cars. I admit I made a lot of

22   money selling Hondas and Toyotas and Nissans. Then I

23   got to thinking about this trade imbalance....

24   *(The following list of trade imbalance statements is*

25   *divided back and forth among all four actors.)*

26   In Japan, everybody gets a cut of the action; this keeps

27   everyone happy and working.

28   In Japan, everybody gets a cut of the action; this makes

29   American goods too expensive to buy.

30   Japan's protectionist policy keeps American goods out.

31   America's open door policy keeps cheap goods flowing in.

32   Japan has beat America at its own game; it's out-capitalized

33   the capitalists.

34   Americans don't want to pay high prices to keep indus-

35   tries at home. They want low prices and cheap third

1	world labor.
2	The average Japanese high school student scores better
3	than the average American college student.
4	American youth have no backbone and are on drugs.
5	Japan is a closed society which does not produce free or
6	imaginative thinkers.
7	Japan is a mimicking society; they copy American
8	technology.
9	Japan doesn't just copy; it makes it better.
10	Americans look for short-term results.
11	Japanese look for long-term results.
12	American industry is poorly managed.
13	Japanese are sinking money into robotics.
14	America's deficit is in the trillions.
15	Japanese work longer hours.
16	Japanese provide better benefits for their employees.
17	America is the biggest debtor nation in the world.
18	The American bond market is supported by the Japanese.
19	Japan doesn't pay for its own defense.
20	America spends too much on defense.
21	America has shoddy merchandise.
22	Japan is a racist country.
23	America is a racist country.
24	Japanese consumers subsidize their foreign markets.
25	The yen is overvalued.
26	The dollar has lost its strength.
27	America for Americans.
28	Japan for Japanese.
29	It's the way of the free market.
30	Americans should stop being crybabies.
31	Americans should compete.
32	Americans should fight.
33	JOE: I was eating a hamburger at the time, and I thought
34	hamburgers could be the answer to the trade imbalance.
35	If I could sell cars, I could sell hamburger. So I threw

1   everything I had into it and set up business here in
2   Tokyo.
3 JIRO: I have with me here my wife. She stays happy all day in
4   this big company house in Torrance. Torrance has
5   Japanese business, Yaohan supermarket, sushi restau-
6   rant, Japanese garden, Japanese language school, and
7   Japanese-American people. However, Torrance is not
8   Japan.
9 JOE: 'Course I did some studying before I came, took a course
10   in Japanese and Japanese business practices, researched
11   the market, read everything. I know if I can make a dent
12   in this imbalance, I'll be doing something. Else we'll lose
13   the trade wars and become an economic satellite of
14   Japan.
15 JIRO: My wife takes care of my mother. That's the way it
16   should be – taking care of your parents when they get
17   old. My wife is very busy this way. This is good activity for
18   her.
19 JOE: I got Michelle and my mother cooped up in this tiny
20   place in Ogikubo. They don't complain 'cuz there's less to
21   clean up after. Michelle and mom are real troopers. They
22   know how important this is to me and to the future.
23 JIRO & JOE: Even when I got to stay out all night. Michelle/Maki
24   never complains. I know I got married to a trooper/old-
25   fashioned type. That is the way it should be.
26
27
28
29
30
31
32
33
34
35

Seer From Saigon

by Elaine Meredith Hazzard

(Scene for an Asian man and woman)

1   Le Yen (pronounced as "Ian") is a Vietnamese teenager, and
2 Dr. Truong is a psychiatrist who has studied abroad and is now
3 practicing in Saigon. The time is the early 1970s, shortly before
4 the fall of Saigon. Yen has been troubled lately because of her
5 increasing psychic abilities which give her sensory experience of
6 the past and the future — of certain people. Her family and
7 acquaintances, failing to understand her gift, regard her as
8 crazy, and her desperate mother has brought her to the hospital
9 for Dr. Truong's evaluation. The locale is Dr. Truong's office.
10
11 DR. TRUONG: You must be Yen. Come in.
12 YEN: I don't want to be here and I have nothing to say to you.
13 DR. TRUONG: Uh-huh. Well, a lot of patients feel that way
14   at first.
15 YEN: I'm not your patient.
16 DR. TRUONG: I find it's the disturbed patients who don't want
17   to talk. Normal people don't have any problem with it.
18 YEN: I would like to leave.
19 DR. TRUONG: I don't think you understand your situation,
20   young lady. You are not the doctor here. And your mother
21   is fed up with your behavior.
22 YEN: So?
23 DR. TRUONG: Your mother is about ready to have you com-
24   mitted. If you don't want to cooperate with me, she may
25   just do that and I won't be able to help you.
26 YEN: Lock me up?
27 DR. TRUONG: I have reports from your teacher, your class-
28   mates. And your mother says you have been a problem at
29   home.
30 YEN: What do you want me to do?
31 DR. TRUONG: Take a seat on the couch and relax. *(She sits.)*
32   I'm really not such a bad fellow as that. And I'll pull my
33   chair around. *(He pulls chair from behind desk and places*
34   *it beside couch.)* And now, let's have a talk. Are you having
35   any trouble sleeping?

1   YEN: No.
2   DR. TRUONG: And when you sleep, do you have dreams?
3   YEN: Yes, I dream.
4   DR. TRUONG: What do you dream about? *(He places his hand*
5   *on her shoulder.)*
6   YEN: *(Facing him)* Not about you.
7   DR. TRUONG: *(Withdrawing his hand, abruptly)* All right, all
8   right. What is it that you dream about?
9   YEN: I dream about my father. I'm worried about him. He's
10   been gone a long time now.
11 DR. TRUONG: And what else do you dream about?
12 YEN: I dreamed about a pink ao dai I saw that I liked. It was
13   too expensive to buy.
14 DR. TRUONG: What else?
15 YEN: I dream that I can fly. It's like swimming through the
16   air. And I want to tell everyone that they can do it, too,
17   that they've just forgotten how —
18 DR. TRUONG: Yes. Flying dreams. They're quite common.
19   And what else?
20 YEN: I don't know.
21 DR. TRUONG: We don't seem to be making any progress.
22   What about a snake? Do you ever dream about snakes?
23 YEN: Not that I remember. Maybe. If I dreamed of one it was
24   probably that I didn't want it to bite me.
25 DR. TRUONG: Men? Do you dream about men?
26 YEN: Sometimes. I guess so. I've dreamed that I met a nice
27   boyfriend.
28 DR. TRUONG: And what did you do with him?
29 YEN: We were walking by a stream. I had my hat on. He took
30   my hat off and he said, "You shouldn't hide your face,
31   Yen." Then I woke up. That's all I remember.
32 DR. TRUONG: Yen, have you become intimate with a man yet?
33 YEN: What kind of question is that?
34 DR. TRUONG: Well, let's say you're a young woman, growing
35   up, and you're starting to have the feelings of an adult

1   woman. Feelings of desire for the body of a man.

2   YEN: *(She stands.)* What are you saying?

3   DR. TRUONG: Let's say you push down these longings to a
4   deeper level. You try to hide them. Say they don't exist.
5   But after awhile, building, these feelings of desire push
6   to the surface and become voices that say things you
7   don't dare think about.

8   YEN: Is that your theory? Are you talking about me or your-
9   self, Doctor?

10 DR. TRUONG: *(He stands, defensive.)* What do you mean?

11 YEN: Where shall I begin? I see you scolding your wife back
12 home. She's nervous. She's afraid of you. "You never do
13 anything right. Why did I marry someone so stupid?"
14 But she knows. You're just covering up. You know a
15 dental assistant. She works right across the street. You
16 take long lunch hours with her at a hotel two blocks
17 from here.

18 DR. TRUONG: What!

19 YEN: And she's not the first one. There have been many. I see
20 many. How many, Doctor? Can you even remember?

21 DR. TRUONG: Stop this!

22 YEN: Your own patients. Three? Four! Four of your own
23 patients. And one of them, not long ago. Two weeks? Two
24 months? She found out she was pregnant. "Get an abor-
25 tion. You're in no mental condition to give birth to a child,
26 let alone to raise one." After you broke it off with her, she
27 cut her wrists with a knife. Blood, on her hands, on her
28 legs, all over the floor. She lost the baby, but she lived.

29 DR. TRUONG: My God! *(He removes his eyeglasses.)*

30 YEN: Were you going to help me like you helped her?

31 DR. TRUONG: How do you know these things? Did she tell you?

32 YEN: No, she never told anyone. She kept your secret. But
33 sometimes, I can see things that happened at another
34 time, as if they're happening right now. I don't control it,
35 it just comes.

1   DR. TRUONG: That's hard to believe. Sit down. *(She leans*
2   *against desk.)* I gather my actions are well-known. Well, it
3   wasn't a crime. That's over with now. That was it. It's too
4   bad it went that far and someone got hurt. But we aren't
5   here to discuss me. It's you who've come with a problem.
6   YEN: And what about the stealing, Doctor?
7   DR. TRUONG: What?
8   YEN: They do still put people in jail for stealing, don't they,
9   Doctor? Even doctors?
10   DR. TRUONG: What do you mean?
11   YEN: The hospital has no idea what you've been up to. They
12   believe you are the good doctor, helping the needy
13   without charge. But I can see, Doctor. Certain patients
14   pay you directly. In cash. You don't give it to the hospital.
15   That's where you got the money for your girlfriends.
16   From the money you steal.
17   DR. TRUONG: You're just guessing.
18   YEN: Am I? How about Mr. Pham, Doctor? And Mrs. Huynh?
19   Remember Mrs. Huynh?
20   DR. TRUONG: How could you —?
21   YEN: Who has to worry about being locked up now, Doctor?
22   *(DR. TRUONG sits on the couch.)*
23   DR. TRUONG: I didn't think anyone would ever know. I used
24   to be a religious man, once. Then came the war. I saw the
25   young men. Post-traumatic shock. Amputations. *(YEN*
26   *sits in DR. TRUONG's chair.)* I didn't think about religion
27   or duty anymore. It didn't matter. I did what I wanted. I
28   didn't want to think about the future.
29   YEN: The Chinese say that once in a village, people came with
30   their problems, the burdens on their back, and laid them
31   down. They walked about, looking at other burdens to try
32   to choose a lighter one. Each one quickly walked back to
33   pick up their own problems.
34   DR. TRUONG: I haven't made a very good job of it. I've hurt
35   people.

1 YEN: I've seen other people do things that were worse.

2 DR. TRUONG: What is it that you want of me? Do you want to

3   see me behind bars?

4 YEN: All I want is for you to tell my mother and everyone else

5   that I am not crazy. That I'm normal, just like everyone

6   else. I'm not going to harm you if you are fair with me.

7   You have your own conscience to live with.

8 DR. TRUONG: All right. I can declare you sane. I can do that.

9   But announce that you are normal, Yen? I don't think

10   that would be in your best interest.

11 YEN: Who are you to declare my best interest?

12 DR. TRUONG: Nobody, Yen, perhaps nobody. But I believe it is

13   better that you face who you are and what you are and

14   come to terms with that, or you will continue to have

15   trouble.

16

17

18

19

20

21

22

23

24

25

26

27

28

29

30

31

32

33

34

35

Yankee Dawg You Die

by Philip Kan Gotanda

(Monolog for an Asian-American man)

1   This monolog is spoken by the character Bradley
2   Yamashita, a Japanese-American actor in his mid to late twen-
3   ties. At this point in the play, he has been telling Vincent Chang,
4   an old Chinese-American stage and screen actor, how important
5   Asian-American role models were to his own development. Of
6   course, later he admits that he was mistaken — that Neil Sedaka
7   wasn't Asian at all. But Bradley uses this incident from his child-
8   hood to explain his need as an Asian-American youngster for
9   legitimate heroes, "and how when you don't have any, just how
10   far you'll go to make them up."

11

12   **It was night.... It was one of those typical summer nights**
13   **in the Valley. The hot, dry heat of the day was gone. Just the**
14   **night air filled with swarming mosquitoes, the sound of those**
15   **irrigation pumps sloshing away. And that peculiar smell that**
16   **comes from those empty fruit crates stacked in the sheds with**
17   **their bits and pieces of apricots still clinging to the sides and**
18   **the bottom. They've been sitting in the moist heat of the**
19   **packing sheds all day long. And by evening they fill the night**
20   **air with that unmistakable pungent odor of sour and sweet**
21   **that only a summer night in the San Joaquin Valley can give**
22   **you. And that night, as with every night, I was lost. And that**
23   **night, as with every night of my life, I was looking for some-**
24   **where, someplace that belonged to me. I took my Dad's car**
25   **'cause I just had to go for a drive. "Where you going, son? We**
26   **got more work to do in the sheds separating out the fruit."**
27   **"Sorry, Dad...." I'd drive out to the Yonemoto's and pick up my**
28   **girl, Bess. Her mother'd say, "Drive carefully and take good**
29   **care of my daughter – she's Pa and me's only girl" "Sure, Mrs.**
30   **Yonemoto...." And I'd drive. Long into the night. Windows**
31   **down, my girl Bess beside me, the radio blasting away.... But it**
32   **continued to escape me – this thing, place, that belonged to**
33   **me.... And then the DJ came on the radio, "Here's a new record**
34   **by a hot new artist, 'Carol,' by Neil Sedaka!" Neil who? Sedaka?**
35   **Did you say, "Sedaka?"** *(His pronunciation gradually becomes*

1 *Japanese.)* Sedaka. Sedaka. Sedaka. *Sedaakaa.* As in my father's
2 cousin's brother-in-law's name, Hiroshi Sedaka? What's that
3 you say – the first Japanese-American rock 'n roll star! Neil
4 Sedaka. That name. I couldn't believe it. Suddenly everything
5 was all right. I was there. Driving in my car, windows down, girl
6 beside me – with a goddamned Buddhahead singing on the
7 radio...Neil Sedaakaa! I knew. I just knew for once, wherever I
8 drove to that night, the road belonged to me.
9
10
11
12
13
14
15
16
17
18
19
20
21
22
23
24
25
26
27
28
29
30
31
32
33
34
35

How I Got That Story

by Amlin Gray

(Scene for an Asian man or
woman, and Caucasian man)

1   The place is Am-bo Land, a fictitious name for the Republic
2   of Vietnam during the years of the American occupation. The
3   central character, identified only as "The Reporter," is a young
4   journalist in his late twenties who has recently been captured by
5   the North Vietnamese Army. In this scene, entitled "Self-
6   Criticism," some of the truths of his situation and profession are
7   brought home to him by an enemy interrogator.
8

9   GUERRILLA: Stand up, please.
10   REPORTER: *(Coming awake)* What?
11   GUERRILLA: Please stand up.
12   REPORTER: It's hard with hands behind the back.
13   GUERRILLA: I will untie them.
14   REPORTER: That's all right. I'll make it. *(With some clumsi-*
15   *ness, he gets to his feet.)* There I am.
16   GUERRILLA: I offered to untie your hands.
17   REPORTER: I'd just as soon you didn't. When you know that
18   you can trust me, then untie my hands. I'd let you take
19   the hood off.
20   GUERRILLA: *(Takes the hood off.)* Tell me why you think that
21   we should trust you.
22   REPORTER: I'm no threat to you. I've never done you any harm.
23   GUERRILLA: No harm?
24   REPORTER: I guess I've wasted your munitions. Part of one
25   of your grenades wound up imbedded in my derriere —
26   my backside.
27   GUERRILLA: I speak French as well as English. You forget —
28   the French were here before you.
29   REPORTER: Yes.
30   GUERRILLA: You told us that you came here as a newsman.
31   REPORTER: Right.
32   GUERRILLA: You worked within the system of our enemies
33   and subject to their interests.
34   REPORTER: Partly subject.
35   GUERRILLA: Yet you say that you have never done us any

1   harm.

2   REPORTER: All I found out as a reporter was that I'd never

3   find out anything.

4   GUERRILLA: Do we pardon an enemy sniper if his marks-

5   manship is poor?

6   REPORTER: Yes, if he's quit the army.

7   GUERRILLA: Ah, yes. You're not a newsman now.

8   REPORTER: That's right.

9   GUERRILLA: What are you?

10   REPORTER: What am I? *(The GUERRILLA is silent.)* I'm what

11   you see.

12   GUERRILLA: What do you do?

13   REPORTER: I live.

14   GUERRILLA: You live?

15   REPORTER: That's all.

16   GUERRILLA: You live in Am-bo Land.

17   REPORTER: I'm here right now.

18   GUERRILLA: Why?

19   REPORTER: Why? You've got me prisoner.

20   GUERRILLA: If you were not a prisoner, you would not be here?

21   REPORTER: No.

22   GUERRILLA: Where would you be?

23   REPORTER: By this time, I'd be back in East Dubuque.

24   GUERRILLA: You were not leaving when we captured you.

25   REPORTER: I was, though. I was leaving soon.

26   GUERRILLA: Soon?

27   REPORTER: Yes.

28   GUERRILLA: When?

29   REPORTER: I don't know exactly. Sometime.

30   GUERRILLA: Sometime.

31   REPORTER: Yes.

32   GUERRILLA: You have no right to be here even for a minute.

33   Not to draw one breath.

34   REPORTER: You have no right to tell me that. I'm here. It's

35   where I am.

1   GUERRILLA: We are a spectacle to you. A land in turmoil.

2   REPORTER: I don't have to lie to you. Yes, that attracts me.

3   GUERRILLA: Yes. You love to see us kill each other.

4   REPORTER: No. I don't.

5   GUERRILLA: You said you didn't have to lie.

6   REPORTER: I'm not. It does — excite me that the stakes are

7   life and death here. It makes everything — intense.

8   GUERRILLA: The stakes cannot be life and death unless some

9   people die.

10 REPORTER: That's true. But I don't make them die. They're

11   dying anyway.

12 GUERRILLA: You just watch.

13 REPORTER: That's right.

14 GUERRILLA: Your standpoint is aesthetic.

15 REPORTER: Yes, all right, yes.

16 GUERRILLA: You enjoy our situation here.

17 REPORTER: I'm filled with pain by things I see.

18 GUERRILLA: And yet you stay.

19 REPORTER: I'm here.

20 GUERRILLA: You are addicted.

21 REPORTER: Say I am, then! I'm addicted! Yes! I've said it! I'm

22   addicted!

23 GUERRILLA: Your position in my country is morbid and deca-

24   dent. It is corrupt, reactionary and bourgeois. You have

25   no right to live here.

26 REPORTER: This is where I live. You can't pass judgment.

27 GUERRILLA: I have not passed judgment. You are useless

28   here. A man must give something in return for the food

29   he eats and the living space he occupies. This is not a

30   moral obligation but a practical necessity in a society

31   where no one is to be exploited.

32 REPORTER: Am-bo Land isn't such a society, is it?

33 GUERRILLA: Not yet.

34 REPORTER: Well, I'm here right now. If you don't like that

35   then I guess you'll have to kill me.

1   GUERRILLA: We would kill you as we pick the insects from
2   the skin of a valuable animal.
3   REPORTER: Go ahead, then. If you're going to kill me, kill me.
4   GUERRILLA: We are not going to kill you.
5   REPORTER: Why not?
6   GUERRILLA: For a reason.
7   REPORTER: What's the reason?
8   GUERRILLA: We have told the leadership of TransPanGlobal-
9   WireService when and where to leave one hundred
10   thousand dollars for your ransom.
11 REPORTER: Ransom? TransPanGlobal?
12 GUERRILLA: Yes.
13 REPORTER: But that's no good. I told you, I don't work there
14   anymore.
15 GUERRILLA: Your former employers have not made the sep-
16   aration public. We have made our offer public. You will
17   not be abandoned in the public view. It would not be
18   good business.
19 REPORTER: *(Truly frightened for the first time in the scene)*
20   Wait, you have to think this out. A hundred thousand dol-
21   lars is too much. It's much too much. You might get ten.
22 GUERRILLA: We have demanded one hundred.
23 REPORTER: They won't pay that. Take ten thousand. That's a
24   lot to you.
25 GUERRILLA: It is. But we have made our offer.
26 REPORTER: Change it. You're just throwing away money. Tell
27   them ten. They'll never pay a hundred thousand.
28 GUERRILLA: We never change a bargaining position we have
29   once set down. This is worth much more than ten thou-
30   sand dollars or a hundred thousand dollars.
31 REPORTER: Please –
32 GUERRILLA: Sit down.
33 REPORTER: *(Obeys. Then quietly)* Please don't kill me.
34 GUERRILLA: Do not beg your life from me. The circumstances
35   grant your life. Your employers will pay. You will live.

1   REPORTER: You sound so sure.

2   GUERRILLA: If we were not sure we would not waste this

3   food on you. *(He pushes the bowl of rice towards the*

4   *REPORTER.)*

5   REPORTER: How soon will I know?

6   GUERRILLA: Soon. Ten days.

7   REPORTER: That's not soon.

8   GUERRILLA: This war has lasted all my life. Ten days is soon.

9   *(Untying the REPORTER's hands)* You will be fed on what

10   our soldiers eat. You will think that we are starving you,

11   but these are the rations on which we march toward our

12   inevitable victory. Eat your rice. In three minutes I will

13   tie you again.

14

15

16

17

18

19

20

21

22

23

24

25

26

27

28

29

30

31

32

33

34

35

CREDITS

BABY JESUS is used by special arrangement with the author, Issac Bedonna. No performance or reading of this work may be given without express permission of the author. Inquiries regarding performance rights should be addressed to the Audrey Skirball-Kenis Theatre, 9478 W. Olympic Blvd., Suite 304, Beverly Hills, CA 90212

ALCHEMY OF DESIRE/DEAD MAN'S BLUES © Copyright, 1994, by Caridad Svich. CAUTION: Professionals and amateurs are hereby warned that ***ALCHEMY OF DESIRE/DEAD MAN'S BLUES*** is subject to a royalty. It is fully protected under the copyright laws of the United States of America, and of all countries covered by the International Copyright Union (including the Dominion of Canada and the rest of the British Commonwealth), and of all countries covered by the Pan-American Copyright Convention and the Universal Copyright Convention, and of all countries with which the United States has reciprocal copyright relations. All rights, including professional, amateur, motion picture, recitation, lecturing, public reading, radio broadcasting, television, video or sound taping, all other forms of mechanical or electronic reproduction, such as information storage and retrieval systems and photocopying, and the rights of translation into foreign languages, are strictly reserved. Particular emphasis is laid upon the question of readings, permission for which must be secured from the Author's agent in writing. Inquiries concerning all rights should be addressed to the Author's agent, The Tantleff Office, Inc., 375 Greenwich Street, Suite 700, New York, NY 10013.

GLEANING/REBUSCA © Copyright, 1991, by Caridad Svich. CAUTION: Professionals and amateurs are hereby warned that ***GLEANING/REBUSCA*** is subject to a royalty. It is fully protected under the copyright laws of the United States of America, and of all countries covered by the International Copyright Union (including the Dominion of Canada and the rest of the British Commonwealth), and of all countries covered by the Pan-American Copyright Convention and the Universal Copyright Convention, and of all countries with which the United States has reciprocal copyright relations. All rights, including professional, amateur, motion picture, recitation, lecturing, public reading, radio broadcasting, television, video or sound taping, all other forms of mechanical or electronic reproduction, such as

213

214

with the author's agent, the Joyce Ketay Agency, 1501 Broadway, Suite 1910, New York, NY 10036. No performance or reading of this work may be given without express permission of the author. Inquiries regarding performance rights should be addressed to the author's agent.

MIJO by Michael Kearns is used by special arrangement with the author, Michael Kearns, 4305 Gateway Ave. #25, Los Angeles, CA 90029. No performance or reading of this work may be given without express permission of the author. Inquiries regarding performance rights should be addressed to the author.

WIPE THAT SMILE is used by special arrangement with the author, Kay M. Osborne, P.O. Box 1587, Highland Park, IL 60035. No performance or reading of this work may be given without express permission of the author. Inquiries regarding performance rights should be addressed to the author.

DOWNPAYMENTS is used by special arrangement with the author, Tracee Lyles, P.O. Box 36423, Los Angeles, CA 90036. No performance or reading of this work may be given without express permission of the author. Inquiries regarding performance rights should be addressed to the author.

LIVE FROM THE EDGE OF OBLIVION, © 1986 by Jerome D. Hairston, is used by special arrangement with the author's agent, Ronald Gwiazda, ROSENSTONE/WENDER, 3 East 48th Street, New York, NY 10017. No performance or reading of this work may be given without express permission of the author. Inquiries regarding performance rights should be addressed to the author's agent.

CAGE RHYTHM © Copyright, 1993, by Kia Corthron. CAUTION: Professionals and amateurs are hereby warned that *CAGE RHYTHM* is subject to a royalty. It is fully protected under the copyright laws of the United States of America, and of all countries covered by the International Copyright Union (including the Dominion of Canada and the rest of the British Commonwealth), and of all countries covered by the Pan-American Copyright Convention and the Universal Copyright Convention, and of all countries with which the United States has reciprocal copyright relations. All rights, including professional, amateur, motion picture, recitation, lecturing, public reading, radio broadcasting, television, video or sound taping, all other forms of mechanical or electronic reproduction, such as information storage and retrieval systems and photocopying, and the rights of translation into foreign languages, are strictly

ment with the author's agent, Judy Boals, of Berman, Boals & Flynn, 225 Lafayette Street #1207, New York, NY 10012. No performance or reading of this work may be given without express permission of the author. Inquiries regarding performance rights should be addressed to the author's agent.

SPIRIT AWAKENING is used by special arrangement with the author, Akuyoe. No performance or reading of this work may be given without express permission of the author. Inquiries regarding performance rights should be addressed to the author, care of Spirit Awakening Foundation, P.O. Box 3722, Santa Monica, CA 90408-3722.

STRUGGLING TRUTHS by Peter Mellencamp is used by special arrangement with the author's agent, Tonda Marton, the Elisabeth Marton Agency, 1 Union Square West, New York, NY 10003. No performance or reading of this work may be given without express permission of the author. Inquiries regarding performance rights should be addressed to the author's agent.

COLUMBUS PARK and *SONGS OF HARMONY* by Karen Huie are used by special arrangement with the author's agent, Vincent Panettiere, 1841 N. Fuller Avenue, Los Angeles, CA 90046. No performance or reading of this work may be given without express permission of the author. Inquiries regarding performance rights should be addressed to the author's agent.

YELLOW FEVER by Rick A. Shiomi is used by special arrangement with the author's agent, Dale Minami, 388 Market Street #1080, San Francisco, CA 94111. No performance or reading of this work may be given without express permission of the author. Inquiries regarding performance rights should be addressed to the author's agent.

TOKYO CARMEN VERSUS L.A. CARMEN is used by special arrangement with the author, Karen Tei Yamashita, c/o Coffee House Press, 27 North Fourth Street, Suite 400, Minneapolis, MN 55401. No performance or reading of this work may be given without express permission of the author. Inquiries regarding performance rights should be addressed to the author.

SEER FROM SAIGON is used by special arrangement with the author, Elaine Meredith Hazzard, P.O. Box 10475, Honolulu, HI 96816. No performance or reading of this work may be given without express permission of the author. Inquiries regarding performance rights should be addressed to the author.

YANKEE DAWG YOU DIE and *BALLAD OF YACHIYO* by

About the Editor

Roger Ellis earned his M.A. in English and Drama from the University of Santa Clara, and his Ph.D. in Dramatic Arts from the University of California at Berkeley. During that time he was also guest stage director for several colleges and universities. He has authored or edited eight books in theatre, plus numerous articles, essays and short stories. In 1991 he initiated an ethnic theatre program at Grand Valley State Univeristy in Michigan, creating guest artist residencies and staging plays celebrating cultural diversity. In addition, he has been director of the University's Shakespeare Festival since 1993. He has worked professionally as an actor or director with various Michigan and California theatres and has served as President of the Theatre Alliance of Michigan for the past six years. He is currently a Professor of Theatre at Grand Valley State University.

Order Form

Meriwether Publishing Ltd.
P.O. Box 7710
Colorado Springs, CO 80933
Telephone: (719) 594-4422
Website: www.meriwetherpublishing.com

Please send me the following books:

_____ **Multicultural Theatre #BK-B205**　　　　$15.95
edited by Roger Ellis
Scenes and monologs by multicultural writers

_____ **Multicultural Theatre II #BK-B223**　　　$15.95
edited by Roger Ellis
Contemporary Hispanic, Asian, and African-American plays

_____ **Plays for Young Audiences**　　　　　　　$16.95
by Max Bush #BK-B131
edited by Roger Ellis
An anthology of widely produced plays for youth

_____ **Scenes and Monologs from the Best**　　$14.95
New Plays #BK-B140
edited by Roger Ellis
An anthology of new American plays

_____ **Audition Monologs for Student Actors**　$15.95
edited by Roger Ellis **#BK-B232**
Selections from contemporary plays

_____ **The Scenebook for Actors #BK-B177**　$15.95
by Dr. Norman A. Bert
Collection of great monologs and dialogs for auditions

_____ **One-Act Plays for Acting Students #BK-B159**　$16.95
by Dr. Norman A. Bert
An anthology of complete one-act plays

These and other fine Meriwether Publishing books are available at
your local bookstore or direct from the publisher. Use the handy
order form on this page.

Name: _____

Organization name: _____

Address: _____

City: _____ State: _____

Zip: _____ Phone: _____

❑ **Check Enclosed**

❑ **Visa or MasterCard #** _____

　　　　　　　　　　　　　　　　　　　Expiration
Signature: _____ *Date:* _____
　　　　(required for Visa/MasterCard orders)

COLORADO RESIDENTS: Please add 3% sales tax.
SHIPPING: Include $2.75 for the first book and 50¢ for each additional book ordered.

❑ *Please send me a copy of your complete catalog of books and plays.*

Order Form

Meriwether Publishing Ltd.
P.O. Box 7710
Colorado Springs, CO 80933
Telephone: (719) 594-4422
Website: www.meriwetherpublishing.com
TM

Please send me the following books:

_____ **Multicultural Theatre #BK-B205** $15.95
edited by Roger Ellis
Scenes and monologs by multicultural writers

_____ **Multicultural Theatre II #BK-B223** $15.95
edited by Roger Ellis
Contemporary Hispanic, Asian, and African-American plays

_____ **Plays for Young Audiences** $16.95
by Max Bush #BK-B131
edited by Roger Ellis
An anthology of widely produced plays for youth

_____ **Scenes and Monologs from the Best** $14.95
New Plays #BK-B140
edited by Roger Ellis
An anthology of new American plays

_____ **Audition Monologs for Student Actors** $15.95
edited by Roger Ellis **#BK-B232**
Selections from contemporary plays

_____ **The Scenebook for Actors #BK-B177** $15.95
by Dr. Norman A. Bert
Collection of great monologs and dialogs for auditions

_____ **One-Act Plays for Acting Students #BK-B159** $16.95
by Dr. Norman A. Bert
An anthology of complete one-act plays

These and other fine Meriwether Publishing books are available at
your local bookstore or direct from the publisher. Use the handy
order form on this page.

Name: _____

Organization name: _____

Address: _____

City: _____ State: _____

Zip: _____ Phone: _____

❑ **Check Enclosed**

❑ **Visa or MasterCard #** _____

                                           Expiration
Signature: _____ *Date:* _____
      (required for Visa/MasterCard orders)

COLORADO RESIDENTS: Please add 3% sales tax.
SHIPPING: Include $2.75 for the first book and 50¢ for each additional book ordered.

❑ *Please send me a copy of your complete catalog of books and plays.*